THE ASYLUM

By CAROL MINTO

with *SUNDAY TIMES BESTSELLING AUTHORS*
ANN and JOE CUSACK

MIRROR BOOKS

MIRROR BOOKS

First published by Mirror Books in 2021

Mirror Books is part of Reach plc

www.mirrorbooks.co.uk

ISBN: 9781913406608

Ebook: 9781913406592

Printed and bound in Great Britain by
CPI Group (UK) Ltd, Croydon, CR0 4YY

A CIP catalogue record for this book is available from the British Library.

I would like to dedicate this book to
my late husband, Sunny.

With thanks to Ann and Joe Cusack

Prologue

Stepping out of the changing rooms, I wrapped the red woollen coat around me and looked in the mirror.

"It looks lovely," smiled the sales assistant. "Just your colour too. It really suits you."

But as I fastened the belt one notch more, I felt a sharp tightening around my waist. My arms and my legs felt as though they were being crushed. It was as though an invisible force was pushing and squeezing my limbs and there was an icy pressure on my throat.

Gasping, choking, I tried to focus on the coat and the mirror and the warm glow of the changing rooms, but it was all nothing more than a red blur.

"Is everything alright?" asked the sales assistant. "You look a bit pale."

She offered me a chair and, uncertainly, I staggered backwards to sit down. Flashing images scattered around me, like falling embers of a firestorm; the needle plunging into my arm, the strait jacket pulling tightly across my chest, the gag stuffed in my mouth.

"'I'll have her – Mackie, the little fair one. Bring her to the treatment room."

I shook my head vigorously, trying to banish the memories, knock them out of my head, once and for all.

"I'm fine, thank you," I said to the assistant with a fixed smile. "I think I just got a bit hot, that's all."

She nodded.

"Well, the coat looks fabulous. I'd treat yourself if I was you. Is it for a special occasion?"

I opened my mouth to reply but again, his face loomed large in my vision; his grey hair, plastered flat and greasy against his head and glistening with too much Brylcreem; his long, pointy nose with a forest of dark hairs up each nostril.

"Your nose is like Concorde," I'd told him cheekily, the thought sneaking out through my lips, like a bubble, before I had chance to snatch it back.

"You're very rude, Mackie," he'd replied, as he dropped the mask lightly over my face. *"And y*ou *have a good imagination, too. But you really shouldn't tell such lies."*

His voice, low and measured, was dripping with scorn and superiority.

"Such lies…"

The truth was out now, of course. It had taken nearly 50 years, but it was out now. And I wasn't the one lying. I wasn't the abuser. I wasn't the monster. And so yes, I suppose this was a special occasion, in a way.

The compensation money meant nothing for the horrors I'd endured. And worse still were the horrors I knew nothing about. But I hoped to put it to good use, buying myself a good winter coat, the sort of clothing I usually couldn't afford. But now, as I unbuckled the belt, and slipped the coat back on the hanger, all I could see was the treatment room. The bare mattress, the syringe on the metal tray, the surgical gloves.

And his eyes, his cold, glassy eyes, leering down at me.

"Poor Mackie, poor little girl, the doctor will make you better now."

Chapter One

Glasgow, Spring 1958

To me, as a four-year-old, the narrow ledge underneath my bedroom window was a relaxing balcony. And it was certainly the nearest I would get. Climbing carefully out of my window, onto my precarious perch, I could already see one of my pals from a neighbouring flat waving excitedly at me from her ledge.

"Hello Molly!" I shouted. "I'm in my pyjamas, are you?"

She was pointing to her own nightie and slippers and starting to shout something about her supper, when I felt a hand yank me by the back of my neck into the bedroom and plonk me on the carpet, legs and arms flailing.

"What the hell do you think you're playing at?" snapped my mother, Rose, 27. "You could fall to your death out there. We're on the third floor, Carol. One slip and you're mincemeat!"

I laughed, amused by the danger and totally unconcerned, like all children, by the element of risk. Mum flapped at me with her hands, about to smack me, but I was quicker than her and darted underneath my bed where she couldn't reach me.

Even after I crawled out, and was tucked up in bed, it was simply a matter of waiting for everything to go quiet, before I would climb out once again, onto my shelf, to wave at my friends.

Our home, on the third floor of a Glasgow tenement on Possil Road, was a happy one. I lived with my parents, my older brother Ian and my little sister Margaret. My Dad, Andrew, was 27 and served as a Lance Corporal in the Highland Light Infantry. He spent months overseas and his homecomings were always something to look forward to and celebrate.

Mum had been a trainee paramedic but had knocked someone down in the street as she was learning to drive an ambulance. Fortunately, the poor man was not badly injured, but it became a standing joke with my Dad.

"She was so keen for her first patient that she knocked him over herself," he would laugh.

Mum lost her confidence after that, and instead worked at the ambulance call centre in Edinburgh. After school, she'd take me and my sister out shopping, and we'd get jelly-babies as a treat if we behaved. In the evenings, before bed, she'd sit us on her knee and read us Bill and Ben books.

But I was forever wriggling away, out of her grasp, always keen to be off playing instead of listening to stories.

"You're a real livewire, Carol," Mum said. "Ants in your pants!"

At weekends, I'd often visit my paternal grandparents, Andrew and Elizabeth, who had a farm outside the city. Gran was small and dainty, strict but loving. Even as a tiny girl, I loved helping out with the cows and sheep. Granddad once sent me out to catch a haggis and I spent ages wandering around the yard, looking under bushes and in trees, until they put me out of my misery and let me in on the joke. When I did finally try haggis I hated it, but I loved the story around it and the image it conjured in my mind, of me poking around the farmyard, wearing wellies three sizes too big, and shouting loudly for a haggis that didn't exist.

Granny was a wonderful cook, and we ate skirlie, a traditional Scottish dish, made from oatmeal and fried with onions and strips of fat. There were clootie dumplings too; a pudding made of syrup, dried fruit and sugar. I always polished off the lot, but was still so skinny and small.

"You need a second helping," smiled Granny. "Or you'll never grow any bigger than me."

We were both tiny and slight, and I liked that. I couldn't think of anyone else I'd rather look like than my beloved Granny. To me, as a little girl, she represented security, warmth, and love.

My brother Ian was rarely allowed to come on those visits to the farm with me, which made that time even more special. He was usually in trouble of some sort and was made to stay at home as a punishment. He was less than two years older than me, so we were close in age, but he was darker, at least a head taller and far wider and stronger. Just as we looked different, our personalities clashed, too. We'd never got on.

"You'll never be able to stand up to that brother of yours if you don't put some meat on your bones," Granny would tell me.

During the winter, he had tried to persuade me to walk out across a frozen pond, but I refused, remembering the dangers my father had warned me about. But Ian wasn't the sort to take no for an answer and he shoved me hard, so that I stumbled onto the ice and skidded a few inches. I screamed as it cracked and I felt myself falling through, into the black icy water below.

Luckily, I was near to the bank and it wasn't deep, so I was able to scramble out. But I was soaked through and shivering violently, my lips and hands blue by the time I arrived home, wailing.

My teeth were chattering uncontrollably, but Ian was right behind me, ready to fill in the gaps in the story before I could even get my breath back.

"She ran out across the pond," he told my mum. "Told her not to."

4

Mum gave me a good hiding, and even when I explained it had been Ian's fault, she didn't believe me, and I got another whack for telling lies.

"You need to learn to behave yourself, young lady," she rapped, as Ian gloated from behind her back.

Another time, Ian had beaten up a local child – younger than him, of course, for he always picked on smaller children – and then he went to tell their parents that it was me. This time, the child insisted that I was not to blame, and her parents believed me. But Mum still gave me a crack across the back of my head, just for good measure.

"That's just in case you were planning anything else," she told me.

Ian would often bully me and my friends, because he was bigger and stronger than any of us. He would follow me out of the house each day and watch everything I did. It was creepy, having him breathe down my neck all day long. I used to think as a child that he hated me, and so he wanted to hurt me. Now I think that he probably had no other friends and followed me around out of desperation, or a weird fascination, more than anything else.

"Mum says I've to keep an eye on you because I'm the eldest," he smirked. "So you're stuck with me."

He would catch Ginny Spinners – our word for Daddy Long Legs – and pull their legs off right in front of me, as I screamed in protest. I wasn't frightened of Ian himself; he was just a big, stupid bully in my eyes, but I was certainly wary of his behaviour. Other times, he would pick up my dolls and throw them hard across the room, so that they hit the wall with a resounding smack. I tried not to react and shrugged as though it didn't bother me one bit. Occasionally, I even threw a doll myself, just to let him know I was equal to the challenge. But after he left the room, I scooped my dollies up in my arms and gently checked them for damage.

"Sorry about that," I whispered into their pink, plastic ears. "You know what he's like."

It wasn't that I wanted to be like Ian, not at all. In fact, I was desperate to be everything that he was not. It helped that we looked nothing like each other; I was small with ginger hair and freckles, whilst he was large, stout and fat, with dark hair and blue eyes. It gave me some comfort that physically we were complete opposites. I hoped that was a metaphor for our characters, too. I wanted, in my child-like way, to put a marker between us, a barrier. I wanted to make him see that I was the antithesis of him, but nevertheless, still a match for him. That he could neither bully me nor boss me around. But I was just a little girl, with a child's view of the world, and could not, in my wildest nightmares, have foreseen what lay in store for me.

*****

In August 1958, before my fifth birthday, Mum made a big announcement.

"We're off to Edinburgh to watch the Edinburgh Military Tattoo," she beamed. "Just you and me, Carol."

She explained Dad would be taking part, playing his bagpipes, along with the rest of the Highland Light Infantry. I didn't really understand what a Military Tattoo was, at that young age. But I was excited, nevertheless. It sounded like fun.

"I can't wait!" I gasped, clapping my hands together.

The week before the Tattoo, Mum and I took the train, all the way to Gretna Green, to buy a kilt for the big occasion. It had to be Mackintosh tartan, in keeping with family tradition, and the nearest place to buy it was Gretna. My kilt, red with a blue and green running through it, was beautiful. I twirled around in the shop and I felt like a Scottish princess. Even better, it was the same as Dad's.

"You'll be like twins," Mum smiled.

On our way home, we stopped off to see my uncle, who lived in Hawick, on the Scottish borders. There was a mountain just behind his house, and sometimes on a sunny day he'd climb to the top and play his bagpipes at the summit. The sound of his pipes, floating down the hill, moved me to tears, even as a little girl. It was magical; it was the sound of home. I just couldn't wait for the big day at the Tattoo, to hear all the bagpipers playing together.

And it got better still, because Ian had set fire to a towel a few days earlier, and so was in disgrace. It was arranged that he would stay at home with a relative, along with my little sister, Margaret, who was too young to enjoy the trip. So it was just me and Mum, off on our own adventure, and as I skipped through the Edinburgh streets, with her hand in mine, I felt a surge of happiness and excitement. She had on her best summer dress and sandals, and her jet black hair, cut into a short, fashionable bob, swung as she walked. I wore my brand-new kilt. I could hardly take my eyes off it and I tripped up a couple of times, because I was too busy admiring the tartan.

"Watch where you're going," Mum admonished, smiling despite herself.

There was a buzz around the city; bunting in the streets, tourists from all over the globe. I thought they had all come to see my daddy. And he was well worth the effort, I was sure of that. It mattered not to me that the Royal Family was in attendance – that even the Queen was there. For me, the real guest of honour was my dad himself.

Of course, the crowds were thick as Granny's vegetable broth and even on tiptoe, I struggled to see anything. And amongst the thousands of soldiers, all in the same get-up of kilts and busbies, all playing bagpipes, I couldn't be sure which one was him. They all looked identical to me. But undeterred, I waved my flag at every soldier that passed. I was bursting with pride.

"Daddy! Daddy!" I yelled.

After the celebrations, which snaked all through the city, Mum and I went for fish and chips, and as a special

Chapter One

treat, we stayed overnight in a cheap B&B. I felt like royalty myself as I pulled the sheets up to my chin that night, the sounds of late-night revellers floating up through the window on the still night air. I imagined that not even the Queen was staying in a hotel quite as nice as mine.

"My dad, the hero," I smiled to myself.

For many months afterwards, and during the evil which followed, I would look back on the Edinburgh Military Tattoo as the best day of my life. A time of joy, of pride, of innocence. And as an adult, just the sound of bagpipes was enough to transport me back to a place of such happiness. In the worst of the trauma, I even bought a CD of bagpipe music. Somehow, it softened my suffering.

Chapter Two

A month after the parade, I started school for the first time, and I wore my kilt proudly every day. By now, we were living in a small house, belonging to the services, on Dudley Drive, Glasgow.

I loved school. I had made lots of friends and by now I was allowed to play out in the street until it got dark. Mum was often out at work or at bingo, sometimes until late in the evening, and my younger sister would be looked after by a relative, so I had free rein to run around as I pleased. Even so, I often wished Mum might get home in time to make me some supper or read a story.

One night, I taped together a few old toilet roll tubes to make bagpipes, and put on my kilt. I found a black woollen hat for a makeshift busby and I marched up and down the living room, blowing on my pretend bagpipes, with my head held high. I gave an imaginary wave to the Royal Family, perched on the sofa. I only wished Mum and Dad could have been there to cheer me along.

The only real trouble came from Ian, and he hung

around like a bad smell, tracing every movement I made. My friends and I spent most of our time trying to give him the slip, running away from him and screaming whenever he loomed into view. Most of the kids on our street were terrified of him; they knew what a temper he had. But for me, he was more of an annoyance. I'd had a beating from him, and I'd survived it, so it no longer filled me with the same fear.

"You're a big bully," I told him, poking out my tongue. "Not scared, not scared!"

Even so, when he lunged at me, I ran away as fast as my little legs would carry me. I was taking no chances.

Just as I had settled in at my new school, Mum announced we were moving to a new house yet again – and this time to Derby, in England. As she delivered the news, my mouth fell open in disbelief.

"What about my pals?" I asked. "What about Granny and Granddad?"

I had lots of aunts and uncles and cousins in Glasgow, too. It felt as though we were leaving an army of support behind. But the decision was made, and so we caught the train, lugging suitcases and bags, all the way to Derby, to a new services' house, a new life. By now, we also had a new baby sister, and she wailed all through the journey. I could only hope that there was no bingo in Derby, and that Mum might be around to tuck me up in bed a little more often.

At first, I missed Glasgow terribly. My heart ached for

Granny's cooking. I even missed the smell of the cows and sheep on the farm. But children adapt so quickly, I soon made new friends at school and there were new adventures to be had. There was a river nearby and when the warmer weather came, we went paddling and swimming.

Ian tormented me just as much, if not more. He would follow me down to the water and jump on unsuspecting frogs, flattening them to an instant and squelchy death. I called him 'Squasher' and the nickname stuck. I was getting older now, I was fiery and more confident, and I stood up for the frogs. I stood up for myself.

"Leave the poor frogs alone," I yelled. "They've done nothing to you."

But Ian threw his head back and laughed, as though my outburst was the icing on the cake in the whole episode. I could see the drool hanging from his teeth as he laughed, and it turned my stomach.

"He's weird, your brother," my pals said. "Really weird."

And they were right. There was no obvious explanation for Ian's behaviour, no starting point. It seemed to me that he had always been difficult, always been cruel. Of course, he was only a child himself and looking back, I have to wonder what he endured, to make him so unpleasant. But at the time, all I cared about was needing to stay out of his way as much as I could. As long as I was out of his punching range, I was safe.

Luckily, there were plenty of distractions, living on the army base. There was a community room where there were regular social events and kids' parties. At Christmas, Santa would come and hand out gifts and there were games and competitions throughout the year.

During the summer months, there was a swarm of kids, buzzing around the base, getting up to mischief and fun. I loved being a part of it all; the army really was like one big family. We were in and out of each other's houses. We were given a cake here, an ice-lolly there, there was a game of hide and seek under someone's bed. There was an easy sense of belonging and familiarity. We got a little dog too, a black and white crossbreed called Peter. I adored him, he followed me everywhere, and often joined in with the mass games of tag we played in the streets.

But at home, cheer was in short supply. Dad was away for months at a time, for so long that on one visit home, I failed to recognise his weather-beaten face and his crinkly smile. I stared at the strange man, standing in the living room, and took a step back.

"It's me, your Da!" he laughed, in his broad Glaswegian accent.

I threw my arms around his neck and cried tears of happiness. He was still my hero, no matter how much he'd changed.

"I've missed you all," he beamed. "It's good to be back."

The visits were golden, but all too soon Dad was packing

his kitbag, ready for his next posting. And it seemed on every visit home, he left Mum with a little something extra. Her stomach swelled, her temper frayed, and the babies just kept on coming.

In addition to me and Ian, we already had two younger sisters, Margaret and Eileen. Then came Steven, one year after Eileen. And before Steven's first birthday, Mum had twins, Lena and Louise. In a little over nine years, Mum had had seven children. She had to give up work, to look after the babies.

Then Dad left the army too, and we moved to a new home, a brand new council house with an inside toilet and bath which, to us kids, seemed incredibly posh. Now he was out of the army, I hoped that Dad might be around more. Life just seemed so much better when he was at home. But his new job was as a lorry driver, and sometimes he could be away for weeks at a time. He was rarely home for more than one night a week and even then, he might sleep for most of it.

"Sorry Carol," he said, as I watched him pack yet another overnight bag. "I have to earn a living, pay for all you bairns."

With every baby that came along, Mum seemed conversely less interested in her family. We could no longer rely on her to cook our meals. Sometimes, it grew dark outside, and we had no idea where she was, less still how we would feed ourselves. She didn't always wash our clothes either. The housework went by the wayside and the place was often filthy, encrusted with dust and dirt.

We were crammed into a three-bedroomed house and space and money were both pitifully lacking. The twin babies slept downstairs in an old drawer. I was in one bedroom with my sisters and Ian and Steven shared the box bedroom. There was a tension in the house, so palpable I could almost smell and taste it. I felt as though something had to give, but as a child, I didn't know what button to push, which adult I could trust.

Mum was out more and more, playing bingo with her friends. She was sometimes out until late at night, and still in bed when we woke the following day. On the days when she wasn't at bingo, she might call the local estate agents and make appointments to view houses for sale – even though she had absolutely no intention or means of buying them. It was madness. It was as if she was searching for excuses to get out of the house and away from her children. Slowly, she seemed to just stop being a mother. She became a peripheral, unreliable, part-time sort of figure. And instead, gradually, much of the responsibility fell to me, as the eldest girl.

I was still only eight years old, yet I learned how to take charge of basic housework. I helped to wake the little ones up for school in the mornings and made them toast, if we had bread in the house. One morning, there was a big fight over a single slice of stale white bread; a free-for-all scrap over the kitchen table. I stood back and watched, overflowing with sympathy at the dreadful situation my younger siblings found themselves in, but also brewing with temper because we were going to be late for school.

"Come on, there's no time to fall out," I chided. "Get your shoes and coats on. We need to go."

And on the school run, again, my emotions collided and conflicted. I wanted to hold their hands, and make sure they were safe. But I also wanted to run along with my own pals. I wanted to be a child myself, yet I wasn't allowed. I thought of my mother, still luxuriating in bed at home, and my face burned with shame and resentment. Why couldn't she take her own children to school? And why was I landed with the job?

In the evenings, we'd often have to cobble together a meal from crisps and sandwiches and again, a row of little faces turned towards mine, expecting me to have the answers. But I didn't know how to cook, and we rarely had decent food in the cupboards anyway. So when Mum wasn't there, I would usually plan a type of indoor picnic, with various snacks laid out on the table. But the excitement of eating jam butties, sitting on the floor and pretending we were on an exotic holiday, soon wore thin.

"I'm still hungry," moaned Eileen.

"Me too," I replied. "But it's not my fault."

The washing, too, was a challenge. We had a dolly tub and a plunger, and though I did my best, I wasn't tall enough to manage the plunger properly. The result was that our clothes were still grubby after washday and often smelled musty or sweaty.

"Not my fault," I said again, as my sisters eyed their clothes with distaste. "I did my best."

The white school socks were the worst, they seemed to show the stains, and I so I would turn them inside out, hoping that nobody would notice how dirty they really were. I burned with shame whenever anyone commented on my grubby clothes. But any criticism did at least serve as a catalyst for Mum to take charge again. She didn't like people passing judgement and so she would wash our clothes, not because she was concerned they were dirty, but because others had noticed they were.

"I won't have the neighbours tittle-tattling about my kids," she said irritably, throwing all our clothes into the dolly tub in temper.

There were occasions when I would fabricate or exaggerate a story about a teacher complaining that I smelled or that my clothes were filthy, just because it was the only way to make Mum take notice.

The housework too, was often my job. When Mum was out, I had to sweep and mop the floors myself, and again, it was a half-hearted attempt, given that the brush was twice the size of me. One day, when I'd finished sweeping the living room, I held the wooden brush handle under my chin and blew into an imaginary bagpipe, whistling a dodgy version of *Amazing Grace* through my teeth. My little sisters laughed when they saw me.

"What are you doing, Carol?" they asked.

"Oh, I'm playing the bagpipes. You won't know what they are," I replied. "It's from a long time ago. That was another life."

And it was true. It really did feel as though Scotland was a chapter from another, happier, life. A distant memory and something which maybe had happened to another girl instead of me. My mother, certainly, had changed completely since then.

Whilst the girls my age were playing out with dollies and prams, I was doing it indoors for real, fussing over the baby twins. We had a banana shaped bottle, with a teat at either end, which I could prop up between the babies and feed them both at once. One day, we ran out of baby milk completely and there wasn't a penny in the house. The twins were bawling, and I knew I couldn't just leave them.

"Alright, alright," I soothed. "I'll sort something out."

I had to go out myself, knocking on doors, until I found a neighbour who was kind enough to help us.

"Here," she said, handing me a tin of dried milk. "This will see you through. But where's your mother? She should be sorting this out."

I thanked her and shrugged. The truth was, I had no idea where my mother was, and I didn't care much either. I wanted her to come home and take over the housework and the childcare. But I didn't actually miss her. Our relationship was already so frayed that I had gone beyond that.

There were some days when I was so busy, or frankly so exhausted, that I didn't go to school at all. We had visits from truancy officers and calls from the headmaster, but somehow, Mum managed to swat away any concerns. One day, a truancy officer knocked at the door and I jumped in alarm, but Mum didn't even flinch.

"Carol's in bed with tonsillitis," she told him smoothly. "Yes, really sick, poor lamb. Can't get to school, sorry."

In reality, I was hidden away in the living room, feeding the twins. One particular officer must have smelled a rat, because he came back, again and again, demanding proof that I was ill. More than once, I heard Mum placating him at the front door, and it would have been easy for me to shout out and expose her lies. But for some reason, I was mute.

Maybe I was protecting the little ones – after all, who would look after them if I had to go to school every day? Or perhaps I was just used to being ignored. Who would listen to me, a slip of a girl with a freckly face and legs so skinny that I couldn't even keep my filthy socks up?

Occasionally, I complained to Mum about the children, *her* children. I didn't like having all the responsibility and none of the fun and, when I got to the end of my tether one day, I told her so.

"It's not fair," I moaned. "Why can't you get up in the

morning and make breakfast? Why can't you take the little ones to school? They're your kids. Not mine!"

But she didn't listen. Worse, she didn't even seem to hear me. Her eyes glazed over, as though there was a glass wall between us. If she replied, I certainly never heard her.

As an adult now, I wonder whether she might have suffered with post-natal depression. Back then it was hardly recognised or acknowledged. Perhaps she needed help and support. But as a child, so did I. And it didn't help that though she hadn't the energy to make our dinners or wash our clothes, she rarely missed her daily bingo fix.

"The bingo matters more than we do!" I shouted one day.

I got a half-hearted clip around the ear for my cheek. Mum rolled out a half-baked excuse about her bad leg, she had an ulcer which often caused her trouble and made her limp.

"I can't take the kids to school, my leg's playing up," she complained. "You'll have to do it. I'm in agony."

But though her bad leg often stopped her looking after us, it never stopped her getting on a bus away from us.

On pay day, she would send me or one of my sisters off to the depot where Dad worked to collect his wages. He was away on a long-haul trip and couldn't pick them up himself. But by the time we saw him next, she had spent the lot.

"These kids cost a bloody fortune," she told him crossly. "I've spent every penny on them."

Chapter Two

As time passed, I resented her more and more. I hated the lies and deceit, I hated the total lack of maternal care. But I knew it was pointless to object. At best, I got a crack across the back of my head. At worst, I was completely ignored. And so, sadly, the little ones took the brunt of my temper, more than once. If I couldn't find the hairbrush, or I'd run out of nappies, or we had no clean school shirts, I often took my sheer frustration out on them. I lashed out with my tongue and sometimes my fists and though I now deeply regret it, I have to remind myself that I was just a child under immense pressure. I was a child playing an adult's role. And because I was a child, I did not question our situation too deeply. After all, it was normal for us, and so I accepted, for the most part, that this was how life was. Maybe all mums played bingo. Maybe all dads worked away. Maybe life was not as rosy and carefree as some of my school pals would have me think. And of course, there were some kids at school who had it much worse than us, and I reminded myself of that, too.

In March 1962, Mum had another daughter, Ava. She was beautiful, and I loved fussing over her. For despite my struggles looking after my younger siblings, I adored them also. I loved dressing them up, especially the twins. I liked bouncing them on my knee, singing *Wind The Bobbin Up* and other nursery rhymes. I was like a little mother hen, old before my time, but clucking contentedly nonetheless. In the nice weather, we'd play in the street, and I kept a close eye on them, rubbing their grazed knees, cuddling away their tears. In the evenings, when it was cold and dark, we played snakes and ladders, and I often indulged them and let them win. That, I imagined, was what a mother was supposed to do.

One day, Louise found a baby pigeon on the path outside, and she insisted on keeping it in the shed in our yard. She grew really attached to it, and when it eventually grew strong enough to fly away and escape the gloom of the shed, she was beside herself.

"I'm not staying here without my pigeon," she announced defiantly, and she packed a bag of clothes and a biscuit and disappeared up the street. She was only a toddler and I knew she wouldn't get far. Even so, I was worried she might come to harm. The minutes dragged by and there was no sign of her.

"I hope she's alright," Eileen said worriedly.

I sighed. I had no choice but to go and find her, sitting at the top of the street, by now regretting the big move. I brought her home, trailing her bag behind her, tearstained, hungry and ready for bed.

"Don't do that again," I told her sternly. "The poor pigeon just wanted to fly away to see his own family."

With an adult around, it would have been a funny incident, but to me, it felt like just another job that I was lumbered with. My mother was out at bingo as usual and had missed the whole escapade.

Chapter Two

On the occasions that Dad came home for an overnight stay, the whole house suddenly seemed to brighten up and snap into life. He usually brought us sweets and we'd tumble onto the floor, play fighting over bags of pear drops and liquorice.

The relief of seeing him there, in the house, was so overwhelming it was tangible. For me, although I loved him dearly, it was about much more than simply seeing my dad. This was my chance to be a child again – and for Mum to be a real mother. For when Dad was home, she would half-heartedly run a duster across the sideboard and she would do some laundry. There was always a home-cooked meal waiting for him, maybe a steak pie and chips or a stew. And of course, because Dad was there, we got the same. Mum was a good cook, but she was also good at putting on a show and at keeping up appearances.

As we tucked into pie, peas and gravy, our mouths and bellies almost singing with appreciation, I was often tempted to shout out and unmask her for what she was.

"Do you know this is the first hot meal we've had all week? Do you know she doesn't even cook most nights?"

But the voice was only in my head. In the end, I said nothing. Nobody wanted to spoil the good mood. We snatched at every strand of joy we could and grasped it tightly. Besides, would Dad even have believed me? Or did he already know what Mum was like? He wasn't a man who looked too deeply into things, and he was neither expressive nor combative. I never knew what he was really thinking. He had a kind, weathered face, and followed the traditional male role as breadwinner, whilst it was Mum's job to raise the children and look after the home. Occasionally, if we were really raising a racket, he would look up from his newspaper with a mild "Behave!" but that was about it. He wasn't a big disciplinarian and he certainly didn't have Mum's quick temper or her barbed tongue. I didn't – couldn't – accept, back then, that Dad had any concept of how we were suffering when he was away. I told myself that he had no idea of the hardship we endured in his absence. I'd given up on one parent and I suppose I simply couldn't face giving up on another.

But all of the signs were there. They must have been. Surely, he realised that we were not properly looked after and that a good wedge of his wages went not on food and heating and clothes, but on bingo? Each time he came home, he was genial and easy-going. He glossed over the cracks, and saw only what he wanted to see. But it would be many years before I could admit that, even to myself.

Chapter Three

After turning 11 at the end of 1964, my thoughts turned to my forthcoming move to high school. For me, the transition seemed somewhat farcical; I had been helping to raise a family and run a home for the past two years. By now, we had two more babies in the family, Clare, born in May 1963, and Alice, in April 1964. There was nothing I didn't know about bottle feeds and nappy changing. I had learned how to throw together a corned beef hash and I could rustle up a pan of stew, too. I had worked out how to separate the whites and colours in the washing. I may have missed a lot of primary school, but I'd certainly had an education of a different kind at home.

Even so, I was looking forward to a new school, along with my pals. With 10 children in the family, life was chaotic and money was more stretched than ever before. We had no telly, no phone, no central heating and yet there were plenty of other households like ours. We didn't feel especially unlucky.

One afternoon, in the spring of 1965, the older kids

were all playing outside, making the most of the first sunshine of the year. The two babies were asleep upstairs. Dad was away working, and Mum was out. By now, she had a job in a shop, but I didn't know whether she was at work or at bingo. I was inside the house, folding washing, enjoying a rare moment of peace and quiet. I was all on my own. Or so I thought. But as I got to the top of the stairs, carrying a pile of fresh laundry, Ian suddenly jumped out from his room onto the landing and grabbed me. The washing went up in the air as I struggled against him.

"Lemme go!" I squealed, more out of annoyance than fright. I thought that this was another of his bullying tactics. My main concern was that I'd have to refold all the washing.

"Stop it!" I yelled again.

But he was far too strong. He was so much bigger and wider than I was, and he towered over me, like a bogeyman. With his hand clamped over my mouth, he dragged me into the box bedroom that he shared with our younger brother. On the walls were posters of Eddie Cochran and Elvis Presley, all Ian's choice. Always his choice. He threw me, like a rag doll, onto the bottom bunk and then pinned me down against the mattress. Frantically, I fought back, trying to shout through the fleshy gag of his hand. But it would have been useless anyway, I knew all the children were outside and the babies couldn't help me. If anything, it would just distress them if I woke them up. It was dawning on me, with a horrifying clarity, that this was more than one of his usual attacks. He sat on me, and then, with his eyes fixed on mine, he pulled off my knickers. A cold, sickly feeling ran right through me like a slick of oil. What was this? What was happening now?

"If you shout out, you'll get it twice as bad," he told me. "Lie still."

He seemed enthusiastic – almost excited – as though he was looking forward to something. In the next moment, I felt a dreadful pain down below, and it was all I could do not to scream. Ian loomed over me, I could smell his biscuity breath, I could see a smile – a laugh even – playing around his mouth.

He removed a spoon – one I recognised from the kitchen – from under my dress and picked up a large spatula from the floor. I hadn't seen those there. I had no idea why he was using kitchen implements to hurt me; it seemed as bizarre and ridiculous as it was cruel.

One by one, he inserted different utensils into me, laughing when I tensed in horror, shushing me angrily if I yelped in pain.

"Please," I whimpered. "Please."

Through the open window, I could hear my sisters playing hopscotch in the street outside, their voices drifting in through the window, carefree and innocent. I could even hear the myna birds, which belonged to our neighbour, swearing loudly. Usually, they made me laugh. Right now,

I felt as though I would never laugh again for the rest of my life.

Ian sat back and relaxed his hold on me and just for a moment, I thought it was over. But then, he unzipped his flies. He stood at the side of the bed and forced my head up and towards his penis. The smell made me gag. To my disgust, he shoved it right into my mouth and I heard him groan ecstatically.

I couldn't breathe.

Tears were streaming down my cheeks, my whole body was screaming silently against it. It seemed to last forever. In reality, I imagine it was no more than a couple of minutes. When he was finished, he issued the same threat:

"If you grass, you'll get it twice as bad."

And then he shoved me hard so that I fell off the bed – my cue to go. He was wiping something off his shoes as I scrambled past him, into my bedroom, with both my groin and my soul crying out in pain. I lay on my bed and buried my face in my hands, and was soon aware of a wet nose, snuffling at my fingers, and climbing onto the bed beside me.

"Peter," I sobbed, cuddling my little dog close.

I knew I could count on him. But nobody else. My mind was a whir with what had just happened. In the bathroom, I scrubbed and scrubbed at my skin until I was raw. I didn't have a toothbrush, I never had, and yet I desperately wanted to get rid of the taste and the sensation inside my mouth.

Instead, I found some antiseptic liquid inside the bathroom cupboard and swilled it around my mouth. It made me retch but anything was better than before. I scrubbed at my tongue with a nail brush until the skin broke. I wanted to go back to bed, to hide away. But it wasn't long before I heard the sound of chatter downstairs and the children came in, wanting food.

On autopilot, I heated up beans and made some toast. As I stirred the beans, I was fixated by the big spoon. I could hardly credit that what had happened to me was actually real. One minute, I was being assaulted with kitchen spoons. The next, I was cooking with them. It was too much for a small child to process and I blocked it out and tried to tell myself it had been a dream. It was my way of coping – the only way I knew. That night, in bed, I refused to let myself think about it. I fixated instead on my new school and all that I had to look forward to.

"It's over now," I reminded myself. "Just forget it."

But just a few days later, the house was empty again thanks to the sunshine. This time, I had no household chores to do, but neither had I the motivation to go out and meet my pals. I felt flat and depressed. As much as I was trying to push out the memories of what had happened, they weighed heavy on me. Eventually, I decided it would do me good to go out for some fresh air, and I went upstairs to find a cardigan. But as my steps reached the landing, Ian pounced once again.

"Keep it shut," he threatened, dragging me into his room.

My entire body was shaking. My heart was so loud in my ears it almost drowned out his voice. It was the same scenario as before, but this time I knew what to expect and so it was far, far worse. The anticipation, as he threw me onto the bed, was unbearable. The sinister line of kitchen implements was ready and waiting. Ian was smiling, almost gloating, as he pulled down my knickers. I had no idea, at the age of 11, that this was sexual abuse – I didn't even know what sex was. But I knew that I hated it.

Ian did not seem to gain any sexual pleasure from the assault; he smirked and smiled broadly. He just seemed to find my pain amusing somehow. It was as though I was a frog, and he was squashing me. As though I was a Daddy Long Legs, and he was pulling off my legs. I felt like I was part of a sick experiment – I was an object, a little project for him. He was simply passing the time. Nothing more.

Thankfully, this time, he did not force me to perform oral sex as before. Perhaps because it was noisy outside, and he feared someone coming in, he stopped, abruptly, after using the kitchen utensils.

"Remember, say nothing," he snarled.

I heard him slam out of the house and then everything went quiet. I waited a while before staggering downstairs, blinded by tears. The younger ones were still playing outside, and the house was empty. I knew I should start cooking a meal – but I couldn't face opening the cutlery drawer and seeing the knives and forks – his instruments of torture – staring back at me. It felt as though they were gloating at me, they were in on the secret. They knew my shame.

"What am I going to do?" I worried out loud. "What am I going to do?"

I knew it would be pointless even to try to speak to my mother. She never listened to me anyway. Dad was always away, and he never really got himself involved in family matters. I couldn't imagine myself discussing such personal issues with either of my parents. It wasn't the done thing back in those days, and especially not in my family. Deep down, I suspect, I also didn't tell Dad because I was scared of the lack of concern he might show. In my child's mind, I had convinced myself that he was a caring and loving father. And I wanted to keep up the façade. I wanted him on his pedestal, for a while longer at least.

All my relatives were in Scotland, and since the move to Derby, we had lost touch. So there was nobody I could tell, nowhere I could turn. I didn't want to stay a second longer in the house. And yet I'd no money to run away – and nowhere to go. Scotland was too far. I had no idea of the way, either.

And even if I did run away – who would look after the little ones? How could I leave them to fend for themselves? It was unthinkable. They looked up to me and relied on me. I couldn't let them down. If I did, I would be no better than my mother, and I recoiled from that comparison.

All these seemingly insurmountable problems stacked up in my young mind, and I felt helpless.

Later that night, Ian came home, reeking of vinegar. I knew he'd had chips. My own belly was rumbling, and I hated him even more in that instant. He was selfish and greedy, to add to all his other faults. I couldn't remember the last time that I, or any of the younger ones, had had chips. Ian didn't have a job, or any money of his own, yet he always seemed to be treating himself to takeaway food.

Despite what had happened, he seemed to behave no differently at all towards me, as he threw his coat over a chair and picked bits of chip out from his teeth. He didn't make eye contact, he didn't talk to me, but then, he never did.

I noticed, as he threw himself on the sofa, that his head was twitching more than usual. Ian had a range of nervous tics, shaking his head slightly, as though he was swatting away an imaginary fly, or stretching out his fingers and pulling them, one by one. After his attacks began, he was twitching and jiggling a lot more. But I knew him well enough to know that wouldn't stop him.

All I could do was pray and hope that the barbaric assaults would fizzle out, and maybe Ian would get bored. But if there was a god, he wasn't listening to me.

"Typical," I thought to myself. "Nobody listens, not even god."

The attacks became a regular torment, twice, maybe three times a week. Sometimes, but not always, I was forced to perform oral sex, with Ian yanking my head so violently I felt he might snap my neck. The kitchen utensils were always there, waiting, under his bed. Afterwards, mysteriously, they found their way back downstairs. Horrified, I scrubbed and bleached them all until my fingers were raw and bloody. But before I knew it, they were back upstairs, ready for more torture sessions. I could see no reason why he had chosen spoons and spatulas to abuse me with. I could see no reason for any of it.

Ian, despite my insistence that he was stupid, was crafty and cunning. He would always wait until the house emptied before he sprang. With 10 children, there was usually someone around, and that saved my bacon more than once I imagine.

Once upon a time, I had encouraged the little ones to play out:

"Get some fresh air! Make the most of the sunshine! See your pals!"

If nothing else, it gave me some peace and it stopped them making so much mess inside. But now, I dreaded them leaving me on my own. I would listen to the glass in the front door rattle, as one by one they all left the house. More than anything, I wished they would stay indoors, and stick to me, like glue.

"See ya Carol, see ya! Won't be late."

"What time's tea? We're going to the park so we might be late."

As the last one left, a hush descended and I was alone. Vulnerable, confused and terrified. I was a sitting target, in my own home – the very place I ought to have felt safe. I was always telling my younger siblings to be careful outside of the house – to be wary of strangers. Yet all along, the evil was right here, in our midst. In our own family. It was so horrific, so outlandish, that I again felt I would never be believed. My brother was a monster, and I had no escape.

That September, I started high school, but the day was overshadowed by the weight of my secret. The tentacles of self-disgust wrapped themselves around my heart, threatening to squeeze the life out of me. For some reason, I felt convinced that this was my fault, this was my doing. I had struggled as hard as I could – as hard as I dared – against Ian. I had done my best to stop it. Yet still, I felt it was my fault. Had I encouraged him in some way? Had I agreed to this, without realising? I racked my brains, wondering where I had gone wrong, and how I could back track to make it stop.

To add to my woes, there was a group of kids at my new school who pointed and laughed when they saw me and teased me because my socks were dirty and my hair was matted.

"Don't stand near her, she's probably got lice," they laughed.

Whenever they spotted me in the playground, they ran away, screaming, as though I was infectious. I already felt grimy and unworthy thanks to Ian. Now, these kids were unwittingly hammering home the point.

"Dirty Carol, she's got the plague," they sniggered.

One morning, in class, my teacher noticed a boil on my neck, and she asked me to roll up the sleeves of my blue school jumper. To my embarrassment, she spotted a similar boil on my arm.

"Dear me," she grimaced. "This won't do at all."

We rarely had hot water at home, so we didn't bath every day. I imagine I had picked up an infection through poor hygiene. I thought perhaps she would tell me off and that would be that.

Instead, she took an instinctive step backwards and frowned.

"I think you'd better see the headmaster," she said nervously, and sent one of the other children out to bring him.

Our headmaster was a large man, whose neck spilled over the top of his tight shirt collars, earning him the nickname 'Fat-neck'. He marched into the classroom, examined the two boils gingerly and then sucked in his breath.

"Looks like scabies," he said authoritatively. "You'd better get your coat and go home."

Behind me, the class erupted into a roar.

"Uggh scabies!" they yelled in delight. "You dirty little cow! Keep away!"

I was usually a resilient child, and certainly I didn't want to give the bullies any sense of satisfaction. But I could not stem the tears as I fled from the classroom, tripping over my feet in my hurry to get away. All the way home, I sobbed. How would I ever live this down? How would I ever return to school? That night, it got even worse, when my best pal, Catherine, who lived on the street, tapped on the front room window.

"I'm not allowed in your house," she told me through the glass. "But I wanted to see if you're OK. They burned your desk and chair after you left, and all your books and stuff. Everything you touched."

I felt miserable, like a pariah. I was the leper of the entire school. Dad came home the following day and he made an appointment with the doctor. And it turned out I didn't have scabies after all, I just had a couple of spots. But the point was made, and the damage was done.

When I returned to school, two weeks later, I was a laughing stock.

"Go to the Mackies and get mucky," sang the children.

Even my teachers eyed me with some mistrust, as though I might be crawling with disease. I never again showed them any emotion. And I knew for certain that I could not confide in them about the abuse. The teachers at school seemed almost as disinterested as my own mother.

And so, as time passed, I built a wall around me, like an armour. To the outside world I was tough and strong, and nothing bothered me. Deep down, of course, I was a frightened little girl, pleading for help and longing for love.

The attacks continued and always followed the same pattern. Ian would grab me at the top of the stairs, drag me into his small room and insert kitchen utensils into me, as I was pinned down on his bunk bed. Sometimes, he would seem almost absent-minded, distracted, as though he was bored by the predictability of it all. Other times, he would laugh in sheer delight at my suffering.

"Tell nobody – or else," he always reminded me.

Afterwards, I would scrub myself vigorously, trying to wash away every last trace of my hateful brother. But his smell, like the memories, was impossible to erase. It lingered stubbornly, like a virus. As the winter months came, bringing with them the bad weather and dark nights, the abuse became more sporadic. Because the children were in the house more often, Ian found it difficult to get me on my own. It ought to have been a relief, but in effect, I became more anxious and on edge. I couldn't adjust to the uncertainty and found it unsettling. And if I went a whole month without an attack there was no sense of reprieve, it just added to my uneasiness that there was one in store, maybe later that day, maybe the following week. Occasionally, I would convince myself that it was over. That he had lost all interest in his perverted games. But it was as if he could read my mind and was toying with me. Because it seemed as though the moment I dared to relax, was the very moment he would pounce.

Other times, I could sense that Ian was about to blow – like a pressure cooker. He ordered the children out of the house, even if it was cold and raining. Mum was out, Dad was away, there was nobody there to defend them.

"Leave them alone," I begged. "Don't be so cruel."

I was pleading for myself, more than them. But they were too scared of Ian to defy him, and they scampered outside as they were told. The silence that then fell on the house was deathly. The stuff of nightmares. Sometimes, my fear was so great, I felt as though my organs were shrinking and withering inside me. More than once, I was so repulsed, so disgusted, that I vomited afterwards.

"What am I going to do?" I fretted, over and over. "How am I going to get away from him?"

Though nobody else knew about the abuse, it certainly had an effect, indirectly, on the people around me. In addition to putting up with Ian's temper, my siblings had to contend with mine, too. I had so much anger bubbling away, under the surface, like hot lava. I couldn't lash out at Ian. I couldn't lash out at my mother. And so, shamefully, my fury was redirected onto my siblings. On one occasion, we were sat around the table and one of my sisters, who suffered with a permanent runny nose, began sniffing loudly and blowing her nose.

"For God's sake. Manners!" I snapped.

She retorted with a quip and I leaned over and hit her as hard as I could in the face. She flinched, stunned, before running away from the table in tears. The look of reproach and disappointment from the younger ones was worse than any punishment I could have received.

Another time, as one of the little ones was refusing to get dressed on a school morning, I picked her up and hooked her onto a spare nail that was sticking out of the wall. Of course, it ripped straight through her pyjama collar and she slipped to the floor, screaming. I felt a flush of guilt and shame. Why was I behaving like a bully, like a monster? I hated this sort of tyranny in Ian, so why was I doing it, too?

"Sorry, sorry," I babbled, knowing my apologies were useless if I kept on repeating the same mistakes.

"It's alright, Carol," she smiled. "I didn't like those pyjamas anyway."

But that wasn't the point. I didn't know what was wrong with me. My temper seemed to rear up from nowhere, like a riptide, and just as deadly. I could not see then that the abuse was causing my anger, that I was confused, scared and damaged. I even felt that it might be the other way round. Perhaps I was being abused specifically because I was angry, because I was dislikeable in some way? Perhaps my anger was some sort of red flag, signalling that I was a suitable victim. I knew there was a link, but I couldn't work out what it was. Even so, my behaviour towards my siblings was appalling and inexcusable. They, after all, had done nothing wrong. They were simply collateral damage in this whole sorry mess. But I was a disturbed child, in a dysfunctional home, and I hope, looking back, they can see that I tried my best. I was sorry then, and I am still sorry now.

Chapter Four

Every single night, from the start of the abuse, I wet the bed. I shared a bed with my sister, Margaret, and so she invariably woke up yelling and complaining. I tried to change the sheets quietly, or just throw a towel over the top, but Mum usually came in and demanded to know what the fuss was about.

"She's done it again!" Margaret complained. "Disgusting! Can't she sleep with someone else?"

Mum changed the bed many times, but never questioned why I was wetting the bed at the age of 12. She never so much as asked me if I had anything on my mind. The only confirmation I got that she'd even registered the problem was a slap on the back of my bare legs.

My fingernails were bitten too, right down to the quick. I had one infection after another in my fingernails, some so rotten and pus-filled that I had to see a doctor for antibiotics. But again, nobody questioned the source of my anxiety. Even my dad, though he saw my fingers bleeding, said nothing.

I also found, to my horror, that I was displaying slight tics – like Ian. I started shaking my head, twitching, from side to side.

"No, no, no," I pleaded. "Not this."

I wanted nothing that linked us at all. I had always found comfort in the fact that he looked nothing like me when we were small – and even less so now. And I wanted none of his attributes, none of his characteristics. Yet the more I tried to rid myself of my tics, the more they plagued me. I would tense my neck muscles, trying my hardest to keep my head absolutely still and fixed in place. But it was impossible; it began wobbling and twitching, all of its own accord. I felt as though he was slowly, insidiously, taking over me, controlling me and ruining me.

One day, early in 1966, aged 12, I took a day off school. There were huge piles of dirty laundry stacked up in the bathroom and I knew we would all soon run out of clothes completely. I used that as my excuse but in truth, I just could not face school. I was struggling to keep my anxiety under control. In class, I worried about my grubby clothes, I worried about my unruly temper, I worried about what we would eat for tea that night. And because I was worrying, the tics would start, and the whole cycle continued.

"A day off will be a good idea," I told myself.

Later, with the housework and washing all done, I pegged the clothes out in the back yard and then waited for the kids to come home. By now, Mum had gone out, taking the youngest ones with her, and the house was empty. Or so I thought.

A few moments later, I heard an ominous click as the front door was locked – from the inside. My heart dropped into my shoes, and my throat tightened. In the doorway stood Ian, his eyes glinting with evil through the gloom of the darkened living room. He nodded to the stairway.

"Now!"

For a moment, I froze. I couldn't run away. I couldn't fight him. Yet I couldn't surrender myself either. My mind was a whirl of panic and contradiction, and in the end, I did nothing. I simply stood and waited as he strode across the living room towards me, as if in slow motion. He yanked me by my arm back across the room and up the stairs, as though I was a scrap of junk. I was so frightened, I thought I was going to be sick again. The anticipation of the torture ahead was almost worse than the act itself. Ruthlessly, he jabbed spoons into me, whilst I bit down on my lip so hard that it bled. Afterwards, I could barely walk. I was in such awful pain, and I felt utterly desolate. I felt as though I couldn't carry on, I couldn't live in this house – and yet – I knew I couldn't walk out on my siblings. I was trapped.

I was still trembling with shock, trying and failing, to see an escape route, when my friend Catherine knocked on the door.

"Why weren't you in school?" she asked. "Is everything OK?"

I realised with a jolt that it was home time, and the kids would soon be back.

"Carol, you look dreadful, what the hell's happened?" she demanded, striding into the hallway.

I tried, desperately, to zip up my emotions, to put up my guard. But it was all too raw. I burst into floods of tears and fell to my knees.

"Come with me," she said firmly. "The little ones will be alright on their own for a while. Let's go the shop. I'll get you a penny chew."

Her kindness touched me. Offering to buy me a penny chew was the nicest thing anyone had done for me in a while. It felt like a huge gesture. On the way, in-between gulps and sobs, the whole ghastly story of the past few months spilled out, like a flood of sewage into the clean air.

"Ian's been touching me, under my clothes," I began.

Catherine's face paled with shock.

"What do you mean?" she asked. "What's going on?"

In a whisper, I told her about him forcing me to give him oral sex and about his weird obsession with kitchen cutlery. Catherine gasped with disbelief.

"What a weirdo," she gasped, shaking her head.

But she had known Ian since we were small, and she was not as stunned as she might have been.

"He's always been evil," she said. "He's made your life a misery. Nothing surprises me with him, he's a freak."

"It's awful, it hurts so much," I told her. "I don't know what I've done to deserve it. I really don't."

"It's not your fault, it's his," she retorted angrily.

As we reached the shop, I pulled my coat around me and shivered.

"I don't know what to do," I told her hopelessly. "I can't put up with this for much longer."

Catherine's response was instant.

"You have to get away," she told me. "You can't stay there, not with that monster. You have to get away."

She said it with such conviction that it suddenly seemed simple, it seemed possible, and I found myself nodding and agreeing.

"That's what I'll do," I decided. "I'll go home and pack a bag. I'll just walk out."

But on our walk back from the shop, a cold reality descended upon me like a damp fog.

"Where do I go?" I asked. "What happens to the little ones? Who will take care of them?"

The same old problems still remained. And Catherine, though she was kindness itself, was just 12 years old, as I was, and between us we had no answers. We had no practical way out.

"Well, maybe you'll think of something," she said encouragingly, as we reached my front door.

I nodded miserably.

"Maybe," I agreed.

In one way, it had been a relief to share my secret at last. Telling Catherine was cathartic, and her support meant a lot to me. I was no longer on my own. Or was I? For in another respect, I felt even more impotent than before. Saying it out loud, admitting it to myself and to her, simply emphasised what a horrific situation I was in. And the fact that neither of us could find a solution to my suffering was soul-destroying.

That night I had a strange dream, that I had written a letter to the police, telling them everything that Ian had done to me. I wrote in big, felt-tip letters: 'My brother is bad' and then I stuffed the folded paper into my pocket, for I had no envelope. Then I rushed outside to deliver it, straight to the police station. I was filled with hope, I had found a solution at last. I would ask the police to help me! I couldn't understand why I hadn't thought of this before. But halfway down the street, I saw a line of policemen coming towards me, almost like an army. It was hard to focus on them at first, because although it had been daytime inside the house, it was pitch dark and late at night outside. And as they got nearer, marching in step, swinging their arms and legs, I realised in fright that they all had the same face – the face of my monster brother.

"I'll take your letter," said one of the Ians, stepping forward robotically out of the line. He moved stiffly, like an action man, as though his arms and legs could be detached. The others stayed in line, staring directly ahead, as though they were under orders not to look at me. I hesitated. I felt uneasy. I didn't want to hand my letter over, but I couldn't think of a reason to decline. I was trapped. The line of Ians was blocking my way and I couldn't get past them, so I had no choice but to hand it over.

"I wanted to post it," I explained nervously. "I wanted to post it through the door of the police station."

Ian nodded his head and solemnly took the letter from my shaking hands.

"Of course," he agreed, before stooping down, and posting it through a gap in the grid at his feet. I listened, defeated, as my letter was swished away, through the drains, and into the sewers. As I turned to run back to the house, I heard the long line of Ians laughing mercilessly, as one. When I awoke, the bed was soaked and stinking of urine, and my nightie was sticking to me. I knew, miserably, that there was no way out. There was no way past Ian.

The summer months ticked around, and with the lighter nights and warmer weather, came Ian's opportunity to step up his attacks once again. I almost grew used to them; I became accepting and passive. Each time it happened, I gripped the blankets underneath me, I screwed my eyes shut, and told myself, silently, that it would soon be over.

"You can do this, Carol, it won't last long. You can do it."

It was as though this was just another part of growing up. I knew it didn't happen in other people's houses.

Catherine had assured me of that, at least. But it happened in mine and I had to live with it. What other choice was there?

And like any child, I was resilient. I was surprised, even back then, at how I coped. I compartmentalised the abuse and never gave it another thought outside of that hideous box bedroom. I played with the twins and cooked and cleaned. My siblings were my salvation. I chastised them and complained about them, but they kept me busy and they kept me going, too. They were a lifeline. Yes, they held me back at home, and prevented my escape. But I needed that purpose, that responsibility. It got me through me each day. They were both my curse and my crutch.

And in spite of the abuse, there was lots of fun. I was naturally a mischief-maker, and I never went for long without a giggle. Catherine and I were forever getting into scrapes. One day at school, I was struggling to concentrate on my maths lesson, and became distracted instead by the girl at the desk in front of me. She had been one of the kids who bullied me after I was sent home with 'scabies', and even now, she turned her nose up at my scruffy clothes. She was forever whispering and raising her eyebrows whenever I walked past. The girl had two long, dark plaits, which reached halfway down her back – and which would, I realised, with a bit of effort and skill – also reach into the inkwell on my desk. Carefully, stealthily, I leaned forward and picked up her plaits. I could feel Catherine willing me on, her eyes shining like an imp's at the desk behind me. Quick as a flash, I dipped the ends of the plaits into the black ink, and of course the unfortunate girl felt the tug and leapt into the air, like a scalded cat, splattering spots of ink everywhere.

"Sit down!" thundered the maths teacher. "What on earth is the matter?"

The girl was shrieking as though her plaits were on fire, and I couldn't contain my laughter. If nothing else, it was a sweet revenge. Of course, I was soon exposed as the culprit and sent to the headmaster for a sharp rap with the cane. But that, to me, was nothing to the brutality I endured at the hands of my sadistic brother. I hardly winced as he brought the stick down on my palm. Certainly, the fun of the crime outweighed the punishment.

"That was brilliant, Carol," Catherine chuckled in the playground at breaktime. "The way she screamed! I've never laughed so much!"

And I was forever getting into trouble at home, too. There was an isolation hospital behind our street, called The Derwent Hospital, where patients were treated for tuberculosis and pneumonia. Around it was a high fence and it seemed, to us kids, to have an air of eerie quiet and malevolence around it. Unlike other hospitals, there were no blaring sirens, no constant stream of visitors, there was none of the usual hustle and bustle.

"What if it's the sort of hospital where they chop up

bodies?" Catherine suggested, and we both squealed in delight and dread.

Waiting until it was dark, we found a broken part of the fence and scrambled into the hospital grounds. Torn between terror and excitement, we crept through the bushes, anxious not to be caught by the staff, but secretly thrilled by the prospect too.

"They might chop you up if they get hold of you," Catherine whispered and we both dissolved into giggles.

It took several trips into the grounds, usually with Peter the dog trotting alongside us for company, before we finally plucked up enough courage to peer in through the hospital windows. To my surprise, I came face to face with a pleasant-looking doctor, in a white coat, carrying a clipboard. In our minds, we'd built up an image of a haunted, deserted hospital, filled with the ghostly screams of patients who had met grisly and untimely ends. But it was, in fact, just a hospital and the doctor, though friendly, looked almost as shocked as I was, as I perched on Catherine's shoulders.

"Run!" I yelled. "Run for it! He's seen us!"

Nobody came after us, we were perfectly safe. But in our haste, we scratched our legs on the fence wire, and when we arrived home, we collapsed in a heap of hysterical laughter.

"That was close," Catherine gasped breathlessly. "We could both have been on a slab in the morgue by now."

That night, I dreamed that I was back at the hospital, looking through the window, but this time Ian's face appeared through the glass. Though I was scared, I reminded myself that he couldn't reach me – not through the window.

"You can't get me!" I gloated.

He didn't reply, and instead walked towards the window, slowly, menacingly, and with such purpose, I felt a chill run through me, even in my dream. When he got to the windowpane, he simply reached through it, and pulled me back through. The hospital ward was small and smelled of sweat and teenage boys. On the walls were posters of the Kinks and on the floor was a battered old pair of boys' shoes… I realised this wasn't a hospital at all. This was the bedroom. The torture chamber.

Why had nobody realised that this was Ian – this was not a doctor after all? I looked around wildly for a nurse or another doctor, someone to help me. How had he managed to con his way in here?

"You're not a doctor," I tried to say. "I'll tell on you."

But though my lips moved, there was no sound. Ian reached deep into the pockets of his white coat and pulled out a large serving spoon and a pair of cooking tongs.

"No," I pleaded. "Please don't. Not here. No."

My mouth opened wide and now I was looking back at myself, at my own, silent scream. I peered down a black hole, into my mouth, and noticed that all of my teeth were covered with the same jagged wire as the fence which surrounded the hospital.

Chapter Five

Mum didn't win very often at all at bingo, or if she did, she certainly didn't share it with us. But one Friday night, she came home in what, for her, was a good mood.

"Go and get us all a bag of chips, Carol," she said, handing me a pound note.

I didn't need telling twice. I ran all the way to the chippie and came home carrying newspaper parcels, soaked through with vinegar and fat. It was the best smell in the world.

"Carol's here with the chips! She's here!" yelled the other kids as I pushed open the front door.

I doled out the packages and we ate them around the fire, out of the newspaper, using our fingers. Each chip tasted divine, they were the best I'd ever had, and everyone agreed.

The twins squabbled over their portions. Eileen told me all about her day at school. Ian wasn't at home, so I didn't need to worry about him. I felt so content, so at ease, as though nothing could hurt me. Best of all, we didn't use any cutlery, no utensils. They stayed in the drawer where they belonged, with all the secrets.

That Sunday, my maternal grandmother visited, and for me it was a green light to go off and see my friends for the day.

"Out to play, all of you," she instructed, shooing us out of the door like little ducklings.

I loved those visits, because I was back to being a teenager again when my grandmother was around. Not only did she take charge of the little ones and the housework, but she also had a galvanising effect on my mother. When Granny visited – which was most Sundays – Mum would make a big effort to tidy the house, organise the kids, and cook us all a hot meal. Any visitor – Dad, Granny, the truancy officer – served as a catalyst to shock her into performing some parental duties. It was such a pitiful shame that her children didn't have the same effect.

That weekend, though, after Friday night chips and a visit from Granny, I felt closer to Mum than I had maybe for years. And I started to wonder if I could confide in her. The abuse had been going on for over a year now, and apart from Catherine, I had told nobody. Perhaps now I could confide in my mother. Maybe I could trust her after all. Nervously, I rehearsed what I might say in my head, over and over. I deliberated over mentioning the kitchen utensils – Catherine had baulked when I had told her that. I didn't want to upset her so much that she refused to hear any more. No, I would simply start with the basic facts and hope she would listen.

Late on Sunday night, I found Mum reading one of her favourite cowboy novels in the living room. The other kids were in bed. Ian was out somewhere, probably up to no good. He had recently been caught, red-handed, thieving from our electric meter. Mum had gone for him, screaming like a banshee. And there were reports among the neighbours that their meters had been robbed, too. All in all, I persuaded myself, this was a good time to speak to Mum.

Even so, as I opened my mouth, I heard Ian's voice, in my ear:

"If you tell anyone, you'll get it twice as bad."

I faltered. What revenge would he take? Really, I couldn't imagine anything worse than what I was going through now.

"Ian's been messing about with me under my clothes," I blurted out suddenly. "He drags me into his bedroom when there's nobody around, he pulls off my knickers and he – "

"Nonsense!" rapped my mother, looking up from her paperback. "Nonsense! He would never do that!"

I stared at her, dumbfounded. I hadn't even finished my sentence before she had shut me down, leapt to his defence, desperate not to hear what she knew to be true.

"How can you say that? You know he's been robbing the meters," I replied.

In my 12-year-old's view of the world, stealing was probably on a par with sexual abuse. Surely she could see that? But Mum shook her head and tutted, as though she couldn't quite believe how outrageous, how impertinent, I was.

"Please," I begged, fat tears rolling down my cheeks and onto my hands. "He puts things inside me. It hurts, Mum. Please…"

This time, Mum slapped her book shut and stood up.

"If there's anymore, you'll get a clip around the ear," she menaced. "Now get out of my sight."

And that was the end of it. I knew I would never again confide her. I knew she was nothing to me.

*****

My 13th birthday rolled around, on December 21, 1966, and then it was Christmas. Money was tight so there was just an orange and some sweets on Christmas morning, for each of us. Mum didn't bother celebrating my birthday at home, but if I was honest, I didn't want her to. I wanted nothing from her. I knew I could never forgive the way she had slapped me down when I had tried to confide in her the most painful and important issue I had ever faced. She hadn't even let me finish my sentence. I would never forget that.

In the springtime, me and two of my sisters were invited

on a holiday for underprivileged children to Skegness. It was arranged through school and so we were told we would have to do our schoolwork there, as usual. But there would also be trips to the arcades, pocket money to spend in the sea-front shops and walks along the beach. I couldn't wait. I really couldn't. It was a massive treat.

"I'm packing a bikini," I announced gaily, even though I didn't have one.

Just the thought of being by the seaside, and being away from home and from my tormenter, was so thrilling. I didn't really care where I went or what I did, as long as Ian and my mother weren't with me. In my mind, the excitement built and built.

But strangely, when I arrived in Skegness on a noisy bus full of excited children, I felt uneasy and unsettled. I was worried about the little ones back at home – how would they manage without me? And even though Ian wasn't here, I had a horrible, inexplicable sense of doom. It was as though I could never escape him – not wholly. Even here at the seaside, when he was miles away, he still had a hold over me. I felt my head jerking and twitching as my dreaded tics surfaced again.

"Why's your head wobbling?" asked one of the other kids. "What's the matter with you?"

"Oh shut up," I retorted. "Just leave me alone."

On the second day, we were given grapefruit for breakfast and I wrinkled my nose in disgust.

"Not eating that," I complained.

One of the instructors at the centre came to ask me what was wrong.

"Don't like it," I said sullenly. "Don't like grapefruit. Don't like it here."

I flounced out of the dining room, suddenly filled with an inexplicable sense of rage and frustration. Outside, I picked up a stone and threw it hard against a window. I didn't really think about it, I certainly hadn't expected the window to smash, but it did. The sound of glass shattering brought everyone running outside. There was chaos, with children and instructors crowding around, pointing at me, and I could do nothing else but admit my guilt.

"Yes, it was me," I said. "Don't know why. I just did it. Sorry."

The instructor shook his head in disappointment.

"Pack your bags," he said sharply.

I was sent home that same day, just two days into the break. I walked out of the centre, hanging my head in shame, and one of the instructors drove me home in aggrieved silence.

I had no idea why I had behaved so badly. Confused and disturbed, I was lashing out at the very people who were trying to help me and show me some understanding. I had so looked forward to the trip, yet I was back home, in disgrace, within 48 hours.

"Doesn't surprise me with you, Carol," huffed Mum

when I landed back on the doorstep. "You're a handful. You're trouble. Always have been. Always will be."

I slammed upstairs to my bedroom and banged the door shut. But her voice, from the staircase, was piercing.

"And don't think you're going to spend the day sulking! There's a pan of potatoes to peel in the kitchen. And then you can scrub the front step."

I stamped downstairs, wishing I had just eaten the grapefruit and stayed in Skegness. No matter where I was, no matter how much I tried, I just couldn't find any peace.

A few months later, Mum announced that she had bought herself a caravan in Skegness.

"Don't tell your dad yet," she threatened us. "Or else."

I remembered my previous trip to Skegness; the smashed window, the trip home in humiliation. It beggared belief that we had been offered the trip out of charity. And now Mum had treated herself to her very own holiday home – in the same town!

"How can we afford a caravan?" I demanded.

But Mum just glared at me. Her lack of empathy and consideration for her own family was jaw-dropping. There was no money for food. No money for Christmas or birthdays. We even qualified for charity-run holidays. And yet our mother led a fanciful life, spending her days at bingo, viewing houses she would never buy, and – this was the ultimate slap in the face – splashing out on a caravan. I had no idea how she had got the money together. Perhaps she'd had a secret win at bingo? There was much about her I did not know – and no longer wanted to know.

Over the years, she and my siblings went to the caravan at various times, Easter, summer, and bank holiday weekends. But I was not invited and nor did I want to go. The idea of being cooped up in a small space with my mother and Ian was horrific. I hated the caravan and all it stood for.

I resented her buying it in the first place, when we were so short of money to live on, and I resented even more that I was not welcome there. It felt like yet another let-down when Ian was chosen to go, over me. What place did he have in the family?

Mum's behaviour in favouring Ian cemented the impression, in my mind, that the abuse was my fault and that I must have done something wrong. Ian seemed untouchable. Each time they were planning a trip, I would hastily let her know that I had no intention of going, before she could tell me I wasn't invited anyway. I didn't want to give her the satisfaction.

"I don't like caravans," I told Mum defiantly. "I'll stay at home."

Instead of being left at home to my own devices, I was instead packed off to stay with my mother's sister, Aunty Bet. She was slightly eccentric but with a big heart, thankfully, nothing like my mother, and lived in the countryside outside Derby in a rambling five bedroomed house, with a large garden and a piano in the drawing room. Aunty Bet was single, had two children, and worked as a lecturer at Nottingham University. My mother was clearly jealous of her.

"She thinks she's a cut above," she said cattily. "University this, university that. All bloody airs and graces."

But I wouldn't have a word said against my aunt. For me, she was the sort of mother I dreamed of having. The warmth and wealth at Aunty Bet's brought into sharp focus the misery and austerity at home. Aunty Bet was a wonderful cook, too.

"We need to feed you up, little Carol," she said.

Her son, Chris, was in his early twenties, and was a gifted musician. He let me loose with his record collection, listening to bands and songs I'd never even heard of. I fell in love with the Everly Brothers through him. Chris smiled when he saw me dancing around the lounge.

"Tell you what, I'll teach you to play the piano," he suggested. "Then you can learn to play your favourite songs."

I stared at him in awe. My experience of older brothers had not been a happy one. In my mind, they were tormenters and abusers. Yet Chris, who was only my cousin, went out of his way to be sweet and kind. He took me into the drawing room and patiently taught me the names of all the notes on the piano. I wasn't used to someone showing such an interest in me and I loved it.

"Come on, budge up," Chris smiled, squeezing onto

the piano seat. "Let's do a duet. You do right hand, I'll do left. We'll put a little concert on for my mum when we get it right."

Sitting at that piano stool, looking out over glorious lawns and a shrubbery, I felt like the Lady of the Manor. I could almost kid myself that this was my house, my piano – and that my life back in Derby was nothing more than a bad dream.

Though she was quirky, Aunty Bet was generous and maternal. Seeing the state of my clothes, she took me out shopping and bought me new outfits.

"Are you sure?" I asked doubtfully, as I twirled around in a changing room, admiring my skirt in the mirror.

"Of course," Aunty Bet beamed. "What else would I spend my money on? You look absolutely gorgeous, Carol, you really do."

I'd never had brand new clothes before and it felt too extravagant. I couldn't shake the feeling that really, I didn't deserve them and I didn't deserve Aunty Bet's kindness. Even as I walked out of the shop, the carrier bag swinging in my hand, I felt a stab of worry, as though this was all wrong. My self-esteem had been chipped away at home to the point where I felt I was literally worthless.

Once, Aunty Bet took me out to a cafe and we had a lovely lunch, with toastie sandwiches and hot chocolate. The cream from the hot chocolate went up my nose and made us both laugh.

"I love coming to stay with you," I told her.

"If you've ever any problems at home, just let me know me," she replied. "You're always welcome to visit me, you know that."

I could never bring myself, despite her openness, to share my secret with her. Whilst I was with Aunty Bet, I didn't even like to think about the abuse, instead pushing it right to the periphery of my mind.

Aunty Bet's was my refuge, my haven. I didn't want to think about my monstrous brother during those golden weekends. But I feel certain, looking back, that she sensed something was wrong. On more than one occasion, she asked me if wanted to confide in her. But I didn't want to spoil my time with her, I didn't want to ruin our happiness. I was grateful for her and our relationship, exactly it as it was. I didn't need any more from her. Yet if it wasn't for my younger siblings – and the worry that they would not cope at home without me – I would have perhaps stayed there for good.

And so, when the rest of my family went to the caravan, I would visit Aunty Bet instead, practise my piano pieces, play in the fresh air, go on shopping trips and outings. I refused to dwell too much on my family enjoying the sea air in Skegness, and hoped it was raining hard on them. It hurt, of course, that Ian was there, and I was not. But I consoled myself that with Aunty Bet, I was loved and wanted and for me, that was a rare feeling.

Chapter Five

*****

At school, it was a year of great change for me and my friends. As we all became teenagers, our bodies hit puberty and slowly, everything began to change. Every conversation we shared seemed to be about boys. My friends had an insatiable desire to know everything about sex and relationships. For me, just the thought of holding hands with a boy turned my stomach.

"Who do you fancy, Carol?" they asked. "Who would you snog? Go on, admit it!"

I shook my head firmly.

"Nobody," I insisted truthfully. "Nobody at all."

It helped that I was a late developer, and so I didn't get involved in discussions about bras and periods and shaving my legs. They didn't apply to me, and I was thankful. I listened, on the periphery as always, an emotional and social outcast, even if only of my own making. I was in a crowded playground, surrounded by children, many of them my friends. Yet I was also completely alone.

Inevitably, as the months went on, the playground discussions turned to sex. In 1967 there was very little sexual education of actual use at school, and so everything we gleaned came from magazines or older sisters and cousins. Again, it was a topic that left me cold with apprehension, but I wasn't sure why.

Then one day, at breaktime, I overheard one of the

girls, more advanced than the rest of us, sharing her latest nuggets of information. She had older sisters and so she was an expert in our eyes.

"It's not just the boy's willy that goes inside you," she said knowledgeably, and clearly enjoying the gasps of awe around her. "It can be a sex aid, like a vibrator. Or a banana! Or anything!"

My blood ran cold. I felt so sick, I struggled to focus on what she said next.

"Ooh, a banana!" said one of my mates, wrinkling her nose in disgust. "Don't fancy it. You don't have to do it, do you? Is that part of sex?"

The first girl laughed.

"Course not," she replied. "You don't have to do anything you don't want to do. If they force you, it's sexual assault. Get 'em locked up for it, dirty perverts."

Still nauseous, I leaned back on the playground fence for support. So that was it. I finally had a name. An explanation. It was a sexual assault. And Ian should, according to my pals, be locked in prison for it.

In one way, it was a relief. I now knew the terminology. And I had confirmation of what I had always known – that it was wrong, desperately wrong, to the point where it was a serious criminal offence. But I was perplexed by the sexual element of what Ian was doing to me. When he was using the kitchen utensils, he never seemed to be sexually aroused, nor did he ever look as though he was enjoying the abuse in a sexual way. The more I learned about sex and sexual stimulation, the less it seemed to fit with what Ian was doing. The abuse was more like an extreme form of bullying. It was a method of control, a stamp of his superiority. Perhaps he got his kicks from seeing me in pain. I would never understand his motives. And even if I did, nothing would excuse them.

But none of this helped towards a solution. I still had no idea how I could stop him. I thought of telling my pals, there and then, in the windy playground. I considered confiding in a teacher – even calling the police. But why would anyone take me seriously, when my own mother had shut me down even before the words had left my mouth? My sense of self-worth was so fractured and fragile, that I truly thought that nobody would listen to me. And even if they did, they wouldn't care less. Because, after all, what did I matter?

The abuse continued that week, the next, and the next. I had vivid dreams, so realistic that I became frightened of falling asleep. In one, I was running away, down the street, towards my school, in nothing but my ragged dirty-white nightie. I knew my mother was behind me, I could hear her screaming my name, increasingly irate. But she had a bad leg and so I was quicker than her, light on my bare feet, and I was soon leaving her behind. I almost felt as though I was floating – was it my euphoria at beating her – or was I actually flying down the ginnels and across the roads?

As I rounded the corner, and whizzed past my school, I suddenly stopped dead with a smack. My face was stinging. At first, I thought I'd hit a brick wall, but then I realised it was 'Fat-neck' the cruel headmaster.

"What have we here?" he smiled, all his yellow teeth on show. "Well, if it's not Carol Mackie with the scabies."

Even though I was dreaming, I could hear my own voice, loud and defiant.

"It wasn't scabies, it wasn't. You burned my desk and there was no need."

And because it was a dream, I added for good measure:

"Do you know what we all call you? Fat-neck!"

I held out my palms expecting a punishment, but instead the headmaster was looking over my shoulder into the mist of the schoolyard, at something I couldn't see. I turned and squinted, and there, emerging from the fog, swinging his bag and smiling broadly, was my brother. My monster.

"Come on home, Carol," said Ian. "I've got something in the bag for you."

I woke, sweating and sobbing.

"It's spoons, he has spoons in the bag," I mumbled. "He has spoons, Mr Fat-neck."

"Carol, you're talking rubbish again," yawned my sister. "You've woken me up and oh, Carol, for god's sake. You've wet the bed."

She sprang up in disgust, suddenly wide awake.

"What's the matter with you?" she demanded. "You're a teenager. Aren't you too old for this?"

She was right, I was far too old to wet the bed. But I was not old enough to cope with most of what was happening in my life. Haunted by the images from my sleep, I changed the sheets and then went downstairs, to sit on my own, in the darkness, until the first shafts of light streaked through the thin curtains. My head nodded and twitched involuntarily, and my nails bled as I gnawed them painfully short.

"What am I going to do?" I fretted. "How am I going to get away from him?"

I asked the same old questions, over and over. Maybe I believed that if I said them often enough, a solution would appear, as if by magic.

Chapter Six

It was not the case, despite the horrors of my home life, that I was a miserable child. Far from it. At school, despite the persistence of a few bullies, I had lots of friends. And at home, though I often resented caring for my siblings, I thrived on the responsibility too. For a child with such low self-confidence, it was the perfect salve to know that I was needed. To know that they could not cope without me.

"Carol, can you lace my shoes? Carol, can you butter my toast? Carol, do you know if I have any clean pyjamas in the laundry basket?"

Their constant demands drove me mad – but I could not have imagined a life without them.

At weekends, I increasingly made time to meet up with my pals and we went off window shopping or getting up to mischief in the hospital grounds.

When the rest of the family went to the caravan, I went to see Aunty Bet to practise my piano. Sometimes, in the school holidays, I'd stay for an entire week. She even allocated me my own bedroom, and I had drawers full of

Chapter Six

clothes there. I had my own toiletries. It felt like a sort of paradise, being at Aunty Bets, as though I had stepped into a magical land.

On the Sundays when Granny visited and took over the household, it allowed me some precious freedom.

"Get out into the fresh air," she would insist. "We don't want rickets in this family!"

Other times, we were packed off to Sunday School. A bus collected us at the bottom of the street and took us off to the church hall. In truth, none of us was really interested in religion, but we went along for the free biscuits and unlimited orange cordial. We'd stuff our pockets with chocolate digestives and custard creams while mumbling our way through the Lord's Prayer. For us, it was a free day out and we looked forward to it.

"I've got enough biscuits in my coat to open my own shop," I giggled, in-between hymns.

Ian never came to Sunday School, so for me, it was a place of sanctuary, in its most basic form. I knew that in church, I was safe from the devil himself. Though Ian was still only 15, he was spiralling into a life of petty crime. After he had been caught stealing from the electric meter, he got into trouble for setting fire to things. I watched more than once, speechless with fright, as he threw bath towels onto our open fire, and they went up in smoke. I was just as upset about the loss of good towels – always in short supply – as the fire risk. When my mother came into the living room, she automatically lashed out at me with her fists.

"What have I told you about keeping away from the fire?" she fumed.

Ian always seemed to get away scot free with a smirk in the background. He was too big now for her to hit him; perhaps she feared he might hit her back. I was still small, and slight – an easier target.

We knew, too, that Ian had a pile of men's belts under his bed, all appropriated from Burtons Menswear. I could never bring myself to go into his room, but my sisters had told me about his stash.

"He's definitely got something else under that bed with the belts," said my little brother. "He goes mad every time I ask him. I don't know what he keeps under there."

I froze, knowing full well what it was. My siblings would have been completely dumbfounded to learn that he was keeping kitchen cutlery under there.

"Probably just more stolen stuff," I said eventually. "Don't think about it."

Sometimes, during the attacks, I would fixate on the belts, wondering how many there were, what colour, what design? I forced myself to run through a list of colours, to focus my mind away from the agony below my waist. He no doubt made himself a few quid from selling on stolen goods, but we certainly never saw a penny of it. I imagined Ian probably spent his money on food; he was obese whilst we were all painfully thin. More than once, I caught him coming out of the pantry with his cheeks and his pockets bulging. Normally, I didn't dare confront Ian. But I was so outraged when I saw him stealing food that I couldn't help myself.

"Oi!" I said. "The food is for all of us. Put some back!"

But of course, he never listened to me. He took what he wanted, I knew that from bitter experience, and food was just another example. If the rest of us went hungry, he certainly didn't mind.

One Saturday, I had been to see Granny with one of my sisters, and on our way home we heard what, to my ears, was heavenly music playing nearby. Not since the bagpipes, in my beloved Scotland, had I heard such a beautiful sound.

"What's that?" I asked, widening my eyes. "Let's go and have a look."

Finding a church door ajar, we crept inside and sat in a pew at the back, listening to a gospel choir rehearsing. The hymns filled my chest with a feeling of joy and peace, to the point where I almost felt I had to get up and sing myself. I found myself humming along. I even sat on my hands, to stop me jumping up and dancing.

It was impossible not to get swept away, impossible to leave the sound behind us. We waited there until the rehearsal was over, when I realised, in panic, that we were late home. My mother was there to cook the evening meal, but we would be expected to help out, to peel vegetables and set the table. By the time we arrived back, my mother was furious.

"Where the hell have you been?" she demanded.

I would have lied to her, I had no qualms about that. Not any more. But my sister insisted on telling the truth and, as Mum's face darkened, I knew I was in for a good hiding.

"That's a black church!" she hissed. "Stay away!"

We both nodded meekly. But even if I had wanted to obey her, I couldn't. The lure of the music drew me back, hypnotically. I sang snippets of the hymns all week, and just remembering the way the choir had swayed and moved made me smile. The next weekend, and the next, I found myself sitting in the back pew, drinking in the music as though it was medicine for my poor wounded soul. In there, I didn't think about Ian. I didn't think about the abuse. I was lifted above it all, to a place where I had never felt so at home.

Chapter Seven

In December 1967, I turned 14, and there was not even a birthday card from my mother. I tried to act as though it didn't bother me, but deep down, I was crushed.

What was wrong with me? She could afford a caravan, so why not a birthday card? She could be nice to Ian, so why not me?

It only added further to my conviction that somehow, the abuse must be my fault. That I must have done or said something to make it happen. And that I was unlovable – even for my own mother. It was a damning indictment for a child to be rejected by her own mother – I realised that myself, despite my tender years. What I failed to realise, however, was that that it was my mother, and not me, who deserved damnation.

The New Year of 1968 rolled around, but my morale was low. I went through my school days and my household chores like a robot, coming alive only when I was playing with my younger siblings, or my friends, or visiting dear Aunty Bet. One day, I arrived home from school to find

Dad at home, sitting at the kitchen table. His face split by a big smile when he spotted me.

"Hello, nuisance," he grinned.

That was his nickname for me. There was always a good atmosphere in the house when Dad was around. And this visit was about to get even better.

"How do you fancy a day off school tomorrow?" he asked me. "Do you want to come with me in the lorry to France?"

My eyes widened.

"France!" I gasped.

Even the word itself sounded exotic. For a moment, I had dreamy visions of the Eiffel Tower and the Sacre-Coeur, even though I knew this would not be a tourist trip. How exciting, France! But then, the images pixelated and splintered as I remembered the little ones. Who would look after them?

"What if I'm needed at home?" I asked quietly.

I couldn't explain the full extent to Dad, that if Mum wasn't around, or was in bed, there was nobody to look after the little ones. Nobody to make sure they had a bath, brushed their teeth, or had clean clothes. I had to just hope he would understand.

"Look, I'm sure Margaret can manage now she's 13," he replied. "And it's only for one night. Might be fun. I'm taking racing pigeons to Calais, you see."

I gasped again. I was thrilled by the idea of seeing the

pigeons fly off, wondering if they would make it back to the UK before we did. And he was right. Margaret was only 11 months younger than me. She was capable of helping out, of course she was.

"Who's going?" I asked warily.

"Just me and you," Dad replied. "A bit of a treat. You work hard, I know that."

I nodded in excitement.

"You're on!" I beamed. "I'll pack my stuff!"

We left early the next morning, before first light. I couldn't help fretting, as I crept in to whisper goodbye to the sleeping twins and the babies. It had become second nature to me to take responsibility, and it didn't feel right, leaving them in the house, even though my mother was in the next room in bed.

"Won't be long, my ducks," I said softly. "Back before you know it."

And as we hit the road, all my apprehension melted away. I loved being high up in the cab; I could see so much, right across the fields and the roads.

"I feel like I'm on top of the world," I announced.

We stopped off at a transport cafe for a fried breakfast, and I was dismayed by the grease and the grime. By then, I was used to keeping a clean house. But that didn't stop me enjoying a sausage butty and a mug of sweet tea.

As Dad drove, we chatted and laughed, and I was so content. We went around the country to various depots, and of course we collected the pigeons, in readiness for their trip to Calais. In some ways, I wanted the journey to last forever. I wanted to stay, perched in that cab, for the rest of my life. With my dad, I felt safe. A little voice, right at the back of my mind, reminded me about the abuse. Suggested to me that this might be the time to confide in my father. But I swatted the voice away angrily. Today was not about that. I didn't want reminders and I didn't want any upset. I was on holiday – I was going abroad – and I was determined to enjoy myself. That night, I slept, cramped up, in a makeshift bed at the back of the cab. Poor Dad slept sitting up in the driver's seat and woke with his head on the steering wheel and a stiff neck!

"I'll be fine," he laughed, rubbing his neck and switching on the engine to warm us up.

It was the one night of my entire childhood, since the age of 11, that I did not wet the bed. That morning, we took the ferry and I stood out on deck, breathing in the salty air. Of course, we didn't see the Eiffel Tower. We didn't even make it to Paris. But that didn't matter one bit.

"Ready for the big race?" Dad asked me, and I nodded in anticipation.

We were on a patch of land overlooking the sea, and the wind was warm. Dad pulled a release lever in the back of his truck and all at once there was a tremendous noise; a flapping of wings and an impatient squawking, as the pigeons flew out of their boxes. As I watched them soaring into the sky, until they were just specks in the distance, I felt my own heart lifting and swelling too.

"Goodbye little pigeons!" I shouted, my face upturned to the skies. "Safe journey back!"

Our journey home to Derby was sombre, and I barely chatted, because I knew I would soon have to face Ian and my mother. But there was a tingle of excitement too, to see the little ones again. And Dad was right. They had coped very well without me – so well in fact that I felt a perverse stab of disappointment. There had been no mishaps, no flashpoints.

"We had meat and potato pie," the twins told me. "Margaret took us to school. She held our hands, all the way, just like you said."

I smiled, but I felt somehow pushed out. It was silly and contrary, I knew. But I couldn't shake it. Had I missed them more than they had missed me? Didn't they need me, after all? Worse, were they even relieved when I was away, perhaps wary of my short fuse? Was it a little holiday for them too, when I was absent? The notion troubled me greatly. Eileen was nine, Steven was eight, and they were very independent. They helped out, too, as Margaret did, with the twins, seven, Ava, six, Clare, five, and Alice, four. I was no longer as indispensable as I had been, or as I thought I had been.

With the summer days of 1968, came the sickening realisation that the abuse had been going on for a little over three years now. It seemed almost unbelievable that I had put up with it for so long. That summer, Ian seemed to take particular pleasure in making me suffer. Perhaps he sensed that, as we both grew older, his time was running out. One or both of us would surely leave home soon. Perhaps he worried that I would find my voice and report him to the police, or to my teachers. Maybe he feared, as I often fantasised, that I would murder him in his bed, and put an end to my torture.

As I matured, I became more acutely and agonisingly aware of exactly how wrong, how very warped, how twisted, it was. As a little girl, I hadn't known what was happening. I had only known I hated it. Now that it had a name, and a context, it sickened me even more. Sometimes, in class, I imagined myself standing up and shouting out loud:

"My brother! My own brother! Has been sexually abusing me for over three years, using kitchen cutlery. He has forced me to give him oral sex. He has threatened me and bullied me into silence."

I could picture the look of sheer disgust and disbelief on my friends' faces. And not just for him. But for me, too, I feared. I was dirty, soiled, imperfect. He had taken away from me all that was pure and innocent. Even now, at nearly 15, I could not countenance even the mention of a boyfriend. I purposely made myself unattractive; letting my hair grow into an unruly mop and taking no interest whatsoever in my clothes or my shoes. Everything I owned, except for those few outfits at Aunty Bet's house, was either a hand-me-down or from a jumble sale, so it wasn't difficult to look untidy.

My pals had relationships, they were by turns either head over heels in love or scorned and heartbroken. There were boys at school who had asked me on dates. Despite my efforts to keep everyone at bay, there were one or two who braved my wrath. But the very thought of even sitting next to a boy made me queasy.

"No," I spluttered. "Never, leave me alone."

I was ruined. Ruined for life. I had accepted that. And so, the summer dragged on, and I dreaded each new day. Of course, over those years of puberty, Ian and I had changed physically and mentally, and so too did the nature of the abuse. He had always been much bigger than me, but now the disparity was more pronounced.

He was far stronger and taller, and he used that to his advantage, becoming increasingly brutal and aggressive. He left pinch marks on my arms and bruises on my thighs. What did not change was the act of abuse itself. Always in the bunk bed, always with kitchen utensils, always wordless except for a brief threat, always horrific. Sometimes he would force me to perform a sex act, other times not.

For my part, as I developed, I gained an insight into the attacks which left me heaving with revulsion. The feelings of injustice and impotence built up inside me, day after day, until I exploded, volcanically. There was nothing I could do to stop those outbursts. One morning, I hit the roof because last night's dirty dishes were still in the sink.

"Why do I have to do everything around here?" I screamed, slamming the pots so hard on the draining board that there were tiny chips flying in all directions. "Why is it always down to me?"

Another time, I flew into a rage because a girl at school said my hair was a mess. I shoved her against the wall in the yard with my hand around her throat.

"What has it got to do with you?" I screamed.

Nobody had any idea why I was so unbalanced. I could go for months, perfectly calm and pleasant, but then the enormity of what was happening to me would hit me without warning, like a car crash, and I erupted. My temper was a sign not of anger, but of fear and distress.

Mostly, my siblings or my friends bore the brunt of my frustrations, and I hated myself for that. They were affected and involved, even though I had tried so desperately to shield them. I was so ashamed of my own shortcomings.

More than anything, I was appalled that I was behaving like my mother. She had a temper and so did I. I became determined to control mine, even in these unbearable circumstances.

There were some days when I could predict Ian's advances. I was better able now to plan and to organise myself, and I could, conceivably, have slipped out of the house unnoticed, and away from his lecherous advances.

But for some reason, I stayed, rooted in place, passive and accepting of my fate. I knew if I escaped this time, he would get me next time, and it would be worse. So what was the point? I was simply putting off the inevitable in order to make my life harder in the long run. And so, I gave up fighting back. In truth, I gave up on myself.

Following my overnight trip to France, I had started to realise, more and more, that the younger kids didn't need me around, certainly not to the same extent as before. And over the summer holidays, they seemed to relish the independence and the freedom, and I had to admit that I was becoming almost redundant.

One afternoon, when the house was empty, Ian took his opportunity to pounce for another attack. I lay on his bed, pinned down with his arm, with my eyes tightly closed, not wanting to see his face. I tried, desperately, to take myself out of the room, like a little bird, fluttering out of the window, back to Scotland, to the soothing sound of the bagpipes, to the Edinburgh Tattoo where I wore my kilt, to Granny's farmyard where I hunted for haggis. Desperately, I tried to dredge those memories up and blot out the horror of the present.

"You'll need a double helping of dinner, Carol," I heard Granny say. "You're such a wee girl."

I strained to hear her voice, to hang onto the vision, but it was blurring and fading. The stench of sweat, and Ian's stale breath as his face hovered over me, snapped me back to reality. When he had finished, he ran a hand through his greasy hair and scooped up the kitchen utensils, as usual, to take them back downstairs. And suddenly, his sheer arrogance sent a flash of rebellion through me.

"You're a dirty pervert!" I shouted angrily. "It's wrong. It's all wrong."

I couldn't believe I had found my voice. But my boldness lasted just a couple of seconds, and then I felt a thwack across my face, so hard it felt metallic. My cheek stung as though he had ripped off a layer of skin.

"Keep it shut," Ian hissed. "Or else."

He slammed out of the bedroom and down the stairs. For some reason, I found myself glued to the bed, as though he was still pinning me down. I wanted to move, but I couldn't. Outside, I could hear the kids playing. It dumbfounded me that life was going on as normal, whilst I was trapped in this hellhole.

I'm not sure how long I lay there, but when I swung my legs over the end of the bed, I had made a decision. I walked along the landing, down the stairs, and out of the front door. I continued walking – with no purpose and no plan. I just had to get away.

"It's wrong, it's wrong, it's wrong," I muttered, over and over again, as though trying to justify to myself why I was running away.

I walked out of our estate, down the main road, past shops, houses and businesses, barely registering my route.

Half an hour later, I found myself at Derby Bus Station. I hadn't consciously planned to end up there and yet it was as good a place as any. I spotted a spare seat in the waiting room, where it was warm and dry, and I huddled up in there for hours, hugging my knees to my chest. My stomach growled with hunger, but I ignored it.

I watched the buses coming and going; people with luggage, people with shopping bags, normal people leading normal lives. So why not me? There were families with children, some my age. I felt crazy with jealousy. I wanted a mum who held my hand, who took me out shopping, who listened when I spoke. I read the destination names on the front of the buses, not all familiar to me, and I daydreamed of a new start. I could hop on one of those buses, and I could simply disappear. I would never have to see Ian again. The tragedy was, I had nowhere to go. No means of escape. Aunt Bet lived in the countryside, she was too far away.

Here I was, in the waiting room, waiting for what? I didn't have money for my bus fare home, never mind about money for a new life.

"Have you no home to go to?" asked a friendly cleaner, as darkness fell. "You're a bit young to be out on your own, duck."

I mumbled something and fled. I had to go back home and face the music, there was no alternative. Mum lost her temper of course, threatening me with a good hiding, reminding me I should have been home to help cook tea and do the household chores. She wanted to know where I had been and so I said sullenly:

"Bus station."

She rolled her eyes as though it was the most ridiculous thing she had ever heard, but never once asked me why I was there, or why I had run away. And I knew better than to try and explain.

Weeks after, the pressure built and built again, and I ran away a second time. This time it was raining, and I had no coat. I was soaked through, but I didn't really notice or care. Again, on autopilot, I found myself at the bus station. The waiting room was at least warm and so I perched on a chair and shivered in my damp clothes. But on this occasion, I had only been there a couple of hours when a young woman came into the room.

"Carol Mackie?" she asked, and I nodded warily.

She introduced herself as Miss Clark and said she was a social worker. Her face was expressionless, like a blank page, but she said sternly: "If you do this again, if you persist in running away, we will have to take you away from your home."

She had no idea how appealing that sounded to me at that moment. She took me to the car park outside and drove me home. On the journey back, she lectured me about the dangers of running away, and about the worry and distress I was causing my mother.

"Oh, she doesn't care about me, one bit," I retorted.

"What makes you say that?" asked Miss Clark.

"My brother, Ian, sexually abuses me and my mum doesn't even believe me," I said. "It's awful. See, I'm safer in the bus station than I am at home."

I heard a sharp intake of breath from the driver's seat. And then nothing. Finally, she said: "We need to have a little chat about this when we get you home."

It was a chink of hope. The possibility, at last, that something was going to change. It was no more than a glimmer, but it shone through the darkness in my mind and I reached out to it.

In the living room, 20 minutes later, it was just me, my mother, and Miss Clark. The other kids had been shooed away outside. Miss Clark shuffled her papers and turned to my mother.

"Your daughter is a fantasist," she announced, all matter of fact. Her features, impassive, seemed still to be set in stone.

"She claims that her brother is abusing her. That sort of thing doesn't happen in families, we all know that. It's simply not true."

My heart hammered against my ribs and there was a ringing in my ears, almost drowning out her voice. How could she dismiss me like that? I wanted to stand up and shout at her, but my legs felt suddenly weak. And I couldn't hear my own voice above the ringing.

"She also has clear issues with anger," continued Miss Clark. "She is exhibiting neurotic behaviour. If she continues to run away, we will have to take her into care. We will have no choice."

I stared at her, and felt a fury boiling inside me, forcing its way up my throat. Suddenly, fiercely, I found my voice.

"Fuck off!" I yelled. "Just fuck off!"

I fled from the room, with my fists balled, and my vision blurry with frustrated tears. How could this happen? Why did nobody believe me? I had confided in my mother. I had confided in the authorities. Nobody listened. Nobody helped. Nobody cared. Ian wasn't even questioned, the social worker hadn't asked to speak to him. She had never actually met him. There was only one possible explanation.

The abuse, somehow, had to be my fault. It always came back to this. I was so unlovable, so dysfunctional, that my own brother thought it was acceptable to sexually abuse me. And my mother and the authorities thought it was acceptable to ignore it.

I did not know what I had done wrong, but I hated myself for it. I wanted to scratch my way out of my own skin, discard my own body and my own character. For I was worthless. Completely without value. Of that, I was sure.

I stayed, slumped on the edge of my bed, until I heard the front door close and the sound of the hateful social worker's car driving away.

"Now you've got social services involved," shouted my mother from the hallway. "Bloody brilliant. This is all your bloody fault."

So that was my fault, too.

*****

In March 1969, Ian ambushed me on the landing for another attack. There was nothing especially different about this, yet the familiarity did not make it any more palatable. He stank of sweat, as usual, and wore a faded black biker T-shirt with 'Road To Hell' appropriately emblazoned across the front. I had stumbled into hell on earth, right here, in a box bedroom in Derby. After he had finished, he vanished without a word, and I broke down into heaving, racking, sobs. I was not getting used to this. I was not becoming immune. If anything, it was all becoming worse.

I opened the window, only with the thought of letting in some fresh air and letting out the putrid air that he had breathed. But as I leaned out, I saw the porch roof below, and without a second thought, I lowered myself onto it. Within a few seconds, I was running down the street.

It gave me a small glow of satisfaction to know that Ian was downstairs, watching TV, and would wonder where on earth I was. I ran and ran, tears blinding my eyes, my nose bubbling with snot. I sprinted down the streets, took a short cut under a tunnel, and arrived at the bus station, almost as though it was my regular haunt. The irony was, I didn't have a penny to go anywhere. It was an illogical choice of destination. But somehow, I felt safer there than at home. I sat on one of the plastic chairs, hugging myself, staring into the distance. The man on the tannoy was busy announcing departures here, there and everywhere. How I wished he would shout one out, just for me.

"Carol Mackie! Excuse me, girl in the waiting room! We've had a free seat on a bus out of here! Destination new life! Anywhere will do! Leaves in five minutes!"

I knew it would never happen. But it didn't hurt to dream. But it wasn't long before I spotted the short, dumpy social worker from last time, marching through the bus station, closely followed by my mother.

"You've gone and done it now," Mum spat. "Come with me."

"Where am I going?" I asked.

"You'll see when we get there," said the social worker. "I did warn you."

I got into the back of her car, sullen and silent. Mum sat in the passenger seat. When we pulled up outside our house, Mum got out, and I opened my door, too.

"Not you," said the social worker firmly. "You're coming with me."

Through the front window, I caught a glimpse of Ian's face. It looked like a smirk, but perhaps it was my imagination. Why was I being removed, and not him?

Chapter Seven

Surely this wasn't my fault? The car drove off through the streets I knew so well, past Bluebell Wood, a place I'd often played with my sisters and my pals. We had built dens there, paddled in streams, had summer picnics. There were so many happy memories. But soon, I was craning my neck and leaving it all behind. Leaving behind my childhood, for good.

Chapter Eight

The Cedars Remand Home was a huge house, unimpressive but somewhat forbidding. There was a red brick wall at the front.

"Right, you'll be staying here," said Miss Clark, as she pulled on the handbrake and gathered up her files.

"Is this because I ran away?" I asked curiously. "Is this my punishment?"

I was quite happy to spend a night or two away from home and away from my family. The Cedars was less than a mile from Bluebell Wood, I had seen it many times when I'd been out playing with my friends, but not given it much thought. I knew only that it was a place for naughty girls, so it didn't concern me.

Miss Clark rapped on the door and I was ushered inside and shown into a little office.

A no-nonsense sort of woman, small and stumpy like Miss Clark, but with short grey hair and glasses, introduced herself as Miss Halliwell. She wore a tweed skirt and a brown blouse.

"I am the Superintendent here at The Cedars," she announced. "I am in charge."

I said nothing. I was starting to think this wasn't such a good idea after all.

"Name?" she said. "Age?"

"I want to go home," I replied.

Perversely, now that I was away, I wanted more than anything to be back. Besides, I didn't have anything with me, not even an overnight bag. I hadn't even let the younger ones know I was going. I hadn't said goodbye to any of my friends.

"I want to go home," I said again.

But I was completely ignored. It was as though she couldn't hear me.

Next, I was taken into a huge room, a long dormitory with around 20 beds lining two walls. The place was chaotic and noisy, milling with girls who were mostly around my age. In fact, as I looked more closely, I recognised two of them straightaway. They lived near me; one was at my school.

"What are you doing here?" I asked.

"No – what are you doing here?" they replied.

I had thought this was a place for runaways, to teach them a lesson. But it turned out that Millie, a girl who lived on my street, hadn't run away. She'd been brought here because of problems at home.

"I have no idea why I'm here," I said, confused.

"Maybe the social workers went to court, to get an order to bring you here," Millie suggested.

I shook my head.

"One minute I was sitting at the bus station, the next I'm here. I don't even have a clean pair of knickers!"

We fell about laughing. Suddenly it didn't feel so bad, despite the uncertainty, because I was with friends. And they didn't seem to think The Cedars was as frightening as I'd feared.

"One thing you should know," Millie told me, conspiratorially. "If the phone rings on a Monday morning at 8am, then you're off to Aston Hall. It often happens with girls who arrive on a Friday evening, like you. I'm just warning you, Carol, that's all."

"What's Aston Hall?" I asked.

"Oh, I'm not exactly sure," said Millie. "I think it's a hotel. Sounds posh, doesn't it? We get girls in here on a Friday, and by Monday, they're off to Aston Hall."

I had to agree, it sounded quite la de da.

"The girls there are given a truth drug," Millie continued.

"A what?" I asked. "What on earth is a truth drug?"

Millie shrugged.

"No idea," she said. "It's just what everyone says. You go there for a truth drug. Probably it makes you tell the truth!"

We both laughed again. Perhaps that wouldn't be a bad

idea, I thought. After all, I wanted the truth to come out. I wanted people to believe me. Maybe this was my chance. I could tell them all about Ian, and something would be done.

"I quite fancy the sound of this Aston Hall place," I said slowly.

But as I lay in bed that night, in a regulation nightdress, I couldn't help worrying about the kids back at home. Nervously, I pulled at my fingers and my head twitched neurotically. I hoped they'd had a hot meal and they were tucked up warm. I missed them.

"You awake there, Carol?" whispered the girl at my side. "Fancy a game of noughts and crosses? I've got a pen and paper here."

Stifling our giggles, we passed the paper back and forth between the beds, and the distraction was a welcome one. I drifted off to sleep with the impression that The Cedars really wasn't so bad after all. The next morning, before breakfast, Millie grabbed my arm and hurried me off down a corridor, both still in our nightdresses and bare feet.

"Where are we going?" I asked.

"The laundry," she said. "We'll get yesterday's clothes back, before anyone else has chance. Otherwise, you end up wearing someone else's knickers and someone else's dress. You have nothing of your own in here, see?"

Together, we rooted through a pile of fresh laundry before recognising our outfits from the previous day. Back in the dormitory, we got dressed and went into the dining hall for a breakfast of stodgy porridge. But there was lots of toast to follow, and big urns of hot tea.

"This place is like a holiday camp," I joked to Millie, as we washed the dishes. "I feel full to bursting."

That afternoon, after the tasks were done, we were given some free time. I was in the dormitory when I heard a commotion outside.

"Carol!" shouted a voice I would know anywhere. "Are you in there, Carol?"

I ran, my heart racing with excitement, to the sash window and flung it open. Outside stood three of my sisters.

"What happened?" they shouted. "Why are you here?"

I stood with my hands on the sill, shouting back an explanation, when suddenly I was aware of a warm breath on the back of my neck. Miss Halliwell reached over my shoulder and slammed the sash window shut – catching the middle finger on my left hand in the process. I let out an enormous yowl, and when I looked down, there was blood everywhere.

"Stupid girl," she said crossly. "You shouldn't be leaning out of the window. Now look what's happened. This is your fault."

My fault. Again. It was clear from the mangled mess at the end of my poor finger that I would need hospital treatment. Miss Halliwell took me herself, complaining all the way what a nuisance I was. At the hospital, my finger was cleaned and bandaged, but the tip was lost forever, probably still stuck on the windowsill, I thought. It was incredibly painful, but I didn't give Miss Halliwell the satisfaction of seeing me cry. I wondered what had happened to my little sisters – they had vanished by the time I went outside with Miss Halliwell to go to hospital. They had probably heard my screams and thought I was being tortured. The idea made me smile. I would set them right, as soon as I was home. It wouldn't be long now.

Back at The Cedars that night, my accident was a cause for more excitement and discussion. And though my finger still stung, I enjoyed telling the story, over and over, in the dormitory. My finger throbbed all through the next day, a Sunday, too. I felt a bit nauseous, and for a few moments, I was homesick.

On Monday morning, as we filed into the dining room, we heard the office phone ringing loudly.

"Bang on 8am," Millie whispered in my ear. "Someone's going to Aston Hall. Someone's off to the hotel."

Miss Halliwell emerged and walked down the line of girls, until she reached me. I felt her hand on my shoulder, and she said quietly:

"No breakfast for you today, Carol Mackie. You'll be leaving us shortly."

My stomach flipped. Millie raised an eyebrow, her face a mixture of dread and excitement. I wanted to go home to see the kids. And if I couldn't go home, I was happy enough at The Cedars for another day or two. I certainly didn't want to go to a new place, on my own. But I was curious about Aston Hall, too. If it was a hotel, or a stately home, it would be worth a visit. It might even be fun. And if there was a truth drug there, I would be believed at last, and it might bring an end to the abuse.

"Aston Hall," I said to myself. "I wonder what all the fuss is about."

I didn't have long to wait. Two social workers arrived, a man and a woman, and I was taken outside to a car.

"See ya, Carol!" shouted my mates from the window. "See ya soon!"

I waved and smiled. I had only been at the remand home for the weekend, and yet I felt already as though I had settled in there and bonded with some of the other girls. It was a funny feeling, almost a wartime-like spirit, pulling together in desperate times.

In the car, I sat on the back seat, quiet with anticipation. The female social worker turned to me from the passenger seat and said:

"Why do you keep running away, Carol? What's wrong with you?"

I adjusted my gaze so that I was looking out of the window, and I said nothing. I had told them once, and I had been vilified for my truthful account. I wouldn't give them another opportunity to do it again. Little by little, the people around me – Ian, my mother, the social workers

– were chipping away at my character, pulling me apart. If I let them continue, there would be nothing of me left. And so, in self-preservation, and no doubt an element of teenage spitefulness, I kept my mouth firmly closed.

"Tell me, Carol," she insisted. "Why do you run away? Why do you tell lies?"

I looked out of the car window, at the neat little houses, the tidy gardens, and I imagined the children behind those windows. The happy families. The love, the warmth, the safety. And I wished, how I wished, that it could be me.

Chapter Nine

The journey to Aston Hall, through Derby city centre and out of the other side towards the village of Aston-on-Trent, was less than half an hour, even in the rush hour traffic. I was still peering out of the car window as we turned into a long, sweeping drive, with a collection of houses and flats on one side. A little further up, we came to a large white house, appropriately named 'Mansion House', with a smart car parked outside.

"Looks like Dr Milner is at home," remarked the female social worker to her colleague.

Further still, we came to a collection of sprawling buildings and took a left, down Maple Drive, past Ash Ward, Oak Ward, and Cherry Ward, until we finally came to a stop outside a sign for Laburnum Ward. At the windows, I could just make out the fuzzy outlines of girls' faces but I was too far away to see any detail. I remember that it struck me as rather nice, using trees a theme.

When the engine was switched off, one of the social workers got out of the car and opened my door. I followed, more inquisitive than apprehensive, as she rang on an old-fashioned pull doorbell. A few moments later, a nurse answered.

"Ah, Sister Clackton," said the social worker briskly. "Here's Carol Mackie."

It was clear that I was expected. The nurse, a brittle blonde in a white hat and dark blue uniform, hurried us inside. Her heels tapped on the solid parquet floor, across the vast entrance hall and through a door on the left, into an office. In the background, I could hear a muffle of girls' voices. I was perplexed. Was this a hospital, or a hotel? It seemed something of a mixture.

We were joined by a second nurse, also with bright blonde hair, who chatted for a few moments, in hushed tones, with the social worker and Sister Clackton. Then, some papers were signed and the social worker left without even acknowledging me. I watched her walk away, with my arms by my sides, unsure of whether I should feel relieved or afraid.

"Follow me, Mackie," instructed Sister Clackton.

I groaned inwardly. Did the use of surnames mean this place was some sort of school? I hoped not. But I didn't have a chance to ask. I was taken out of the office, up a flight of concrete stairs, and through what looked exactly like a hospital ward. There were rows of iron hospital beds on either wall. Why on earth was I in hospital, I wondered? There was absolutely nothing wrong with me. But Sister

Clackton was bustling ahead, clearly in no mood for questions, so I followed obediently. At the far end of the ward we arrived at a heavy door with a long line of locks down the side. My skin prickled.

"Just like a prison door," I said to myself.

Sister Clackton jiggled a set of keys and the door swung open. She led me into a small room. There was a single mattress on the floor, and a small window on one wall. But there was nothing else. I could clearly hear the girls' voices now, a low hub of chatter, possibly coming from the floor below. But in the room itself, it was silent. Deathly.

I blushed a little as my stomach growled, a reminder that I'd had no breakfast – not even a drink of water. I was desperately hungry and thirsty, but so far, nobody had said a word to me. All the conversation had been about me, but not including me.

"Could I maybe have something to eat?" I asked politely. "I've had no breakfast, see."

Nurse Clackton shook her head without looking at me.

"A cup of tea?" I said hopefully. "Orange squash maybe?"

She shook her head again.

"Nothing at all, I'm afraid," she said, sounding not in the least bit sympathetic. "Now, can you take off your clothes, everything please."

I recoiled.

"Everything? Why?"

But Nurse Clackton simply pursed her lips and said: "Everything. Quickly."

I was as self-conscious as any 15-year-old girl and the idea of stripping off in front of a complete stranger was alarming. And though she was a nurse, I felt a distinct sense of mistrust and bewilderment. I felt certain that there must be some mix-up, because none of this made sense. I wasn't ill at all, and yet I was seemingly in a hospital, and probably about to have some sort of examination.

"I'm not ill," I said in a small voice. "There's nothing wrong with me. I'm just hungry. I don't need to get undressed, do I?"

But the way Sister Clackton glowered at me left me with little alternative but to comply. My skin tingled as I stood naked in front of her, shivering with both cold and embarrassment.

"Lie on the mattress," she instructed.

Then, she picked up what looked like a white, short-sleeved coat, with long straps and buckles hanging off it.

"Keep still," she ordered, as she sat me up and strapped me into the coat, tying my arms, and then my legs, firmly together. Panic rushed through me and my heart thumped. I couldn't move. Not at all. I had a sudden flashback to being held down on the bunkbed, Ian's weight squashing me, crushing my spirit. Was this a trap – was I being trussed up, ready for my brother to come in and abuse me? Was this nurse part of the whole conspiracy?

"What's going on?" I babbled. "I'm not ill. I've never been ill. This is not right."

But she said nothing. She stood back to survey her handiwork, and then left the room, leaving me bound, helpless and scared witless. I struggled and struggled but the buckles were tight. My arms were tied together, at the front. I seemed to be strapped into something that was a cross between a strait jacket and a padded hospital gown. For some reason, it stank of oil. The smell, hitting my empty stomach, made me want to vomit. I lay, petrified, for what felt like ages but in reality was perhaps half an hour.

I wondered, wildly, if I was going to be murdered or even sacrificed as part of some bizarre ritual. Whether these were my last breaths… Or was Ian on his way here, right now, bringing with him his perverted collection of serving spoons, spatulas and fish slices? I shuddered. What would be worse? Though I wasn't gagged, instinctively, I felt it wise to stay silent. I was too scared to scream for help; too scared of who might answer my cries.

When the door opened again, Sister Clackton came in, carrying a metal tray. From my prone position on the mattress I couldn't see what was on it, but there was a faint, metallic rattle, as though it held surgical instruments of some sort. In that moment, in my mind's eye, I saw a malevolent flash of a kitchen spoon. Then a grisly spatula. Was it going to happen again? Same utensils, different attacker?

"Please, no," I muttered. "Don't do it again."

Behind Sister Clackton, a man with a grey suit, grey hair and dark rimmed glasses followed. He was virtually monochrome, as though he had just stepped right out of a black and white telly. I had never seen him before but instantly, I was petrified.

"Now, Carol Mackie, little Carol Mackie," he said softly.

His voice was oily and creepy. He stood over me and I cringed. I felt myself visibly shrinking. My only comfort was that the jacket was long enough to cover my private parts. In fact it almost reached my knees, but still, I felt horribly exposed and vulnerable, yet trussed and trapped. As his face loomed, I had another flashback, to Ian.

"No, please, no," I murmured again.

The man sat down on the edge of the mattress, so that his thigh was touching my leg. I shivered. I knew now what it was. I knew what was coming. This was my fault. My fault for being angry. My fault for being abused. If, in that moment, I could have chosen to die to escape my punishment, I would have.

"F*** off!" I spat, my fear spilling over.

The man raised his eyebrows in mild surprise.

"You can't talk to me like that," he said. "I'm Dr Milner, I'm the Physician Superintendent of Aston Hall."

The words were a welcome shock. I'd had no idea he was a doctor. Perhaps he was here to help me after all. But then he nodded towards Sister Clackton and she handed him a syringe from her ghastly tray. Again, fear coursed through my body. Was this the end of me? He rubbed the inside of my forearm slightly, before plunging the needle into my vein. In the seconds afterwards, I had the peculiar sensation that I was frozen, both icy cold and paralysed. I was clamped to the bed, as if by invisible manacles and my arms and legs felt so heavy. So terribly heavy.

"So," said Dr Milner, standing up after the injection was finished. "Tell me why you ran away, Carol."

Despite myself, I heard my voice telling him the truth.

"My brother has been abusing me sexually, for years," I replied, hot, humiliated tears pricking at my eyes and rolling down my cheeks. Curiously, as they dripped from my face, I felt nothing as they splashed onto my shoulders.

Dr Milner sighed, a little irritated, perhaps. I couldn't tell. "Are you sure, Carol", he asked. "Are you absolutely sure?"

"Of course I am," I wept. "I wouldn't say it if it wasn't true."

I told him all about Ian, about the kitchen utensils, about the oral sex, about my desperation for it to stop, and for my account of the abuse to be believed.

"Are you sure?" Milner pressed again. "Absolutely sure?"

"Yes!" I shouted, but my voice was somehow thin and pathetic.

"It's not good to tell lies," Milner said, pacing the small room, back and forth, back and forth. "Not good, Carol."

Another one, I thought. Another one who doesn't believe me. I was conscious, but sluggish. The room seemed distant somehow, and Milner's voice, the next time he spoke, came from the far end of a long, dark tunnel.

"You're a naughty girl, he said, with a stain of a smile playing around the edges of his lips.

I felt sick and uneasy. I had the feeling he was planning something else. But what? Despite my drowsiness, I fought to stay awake. I focussed on his face and made myself take in every feature.

"You have a nose like Concorde," I blurted suddenly, the words escaping my lips before I could snatch them back.

Milner shook his head and tutted, as if he had his work cut out with me.

"We will leave it there for today," he said sorrowfully, and I got the impression I had disappointed him somehow. I had a moment of promise, where I felt he might release me. But it was swiftly and cruelly stolen from me. Milner took a scrap of gauze off the tray, left behind by Sister Clackton, and dropped it casually over my face, almost as though it was a piece of litter. Then he squeezed several droplets onto the gauze, and I was overwhelmed with a feeling of intense nausea and exhaustion. I was dragged backwards, downwards, into the abyss. Into the darkness.

*****

When I awoke, groggy and disorientated, it was night-time. I was rigid, cold and scared. My mind a jumble of jagged and unrelated thoughts. My body was heavy and aching and down below, I had a stinging sensation. I was bleeding too, and I could feel something wet between my legs. Though I was alone in the room, I knew that somebody must have been in here with me. I was determined not to crack, but it was no good. No matter how tightly I shut my eyes, the tears leaked through. Grief for what I had already suffered. Terror for what lay ahead.

Chapter Ten

It could have been minutes or hours: I had no idea how long I lay on the mattress. But eventually, the door opened, and Sister Clackton was standing over me.

"Time to go to the ward," she said.

As she busied herself, untying my hands and feet, all I could think about was the searing pain between my legs. I'd had this before – after the abuse by Ian, though this time, it felt much worse, much sharper. I was still bleeding too, spots here and there on the insides of my thighs. I knew I had been violated in some way. But I didn't dare ask Sister Clackton what had happened. And anyway, I didn't really want the answers.

"Come on," she said crisply. "Don't dawdle, Mackie."

We went back to the ward I'd seen the previous day, but this time, she showed me to a bed, roughly halfway along the wall.

"Get into bed," she said. "And don't get out."

Wearily, I clambered into bed, underneath cold, stiff sheets. It was quiet, eerily so. The ward was old-fashioned, decrepit even, with peeling paint on the walls behind me and a soft rattle from the windows where the draft seeped in. There was a strong, almost overpowering smell of disinfectant, and under it, the faint stench of urine. I was still drowsy and disorientated and, despite my uneasiness, I felt myself drifting off into an unsettled sleep with dreams of long, ghostly fingers prodding and poking me so hard that I felt my face begin to fold in on itself, disintegrating, crumbling and pixelating, little by little, piece by piece. The fingers scratched and ripped at my skin until my entire face had fallen apart and all that remained was a pile of fragments, as though I was an incomplete jigsaw. My identity, my very being, had been obliterated.

"Ha, Mackie, you're in a mess now," screamed the voice behind the ghostly fingers. "You're never going home. Never!"

She wore the same white hat and blue uniform as Sister Clackton and tucked into her pocket was a big syringe. But when she turned her face towards me, I realised it was my own treacherous mother. I tried to scream, but my mouth was in small pieces on the floor, and I couldn't make a sound.

Hours later, when I woke, I could hear the distant, muted chatter of teenage girls. I remembered hearing that same sound when I had first arrived here. I looked around me at 21 empty beds, and I realised the faceless voices below me would probably fill these beds later. In the pit of my stomach, I felt anxious. Were those girls part of the plot? Would they attack me, too? At some point, as I lapsed in and out of consciousness, a nurse swung through the doors, pushing a trolley, with a plate of stew and a glass of water on it. The meaty smell, mixed in with disinfectant, made me want to retch. I was so weak and hungry; I could hear my stomach complaining loudly. I didn't know what time it was, but I was sure I hadn't eaten for well over 24 hours. But I felt sickly too. I wasn't sure I could even swallow.

"Get this down you," said the nurse, not unkindly, handing me the lamb stew. "It will do you good."

I had to force down the first few mouthfuls, but it was so tasty that I soon finished the lot. The nurse returned later, to take away my dirty plate and cup, and she smiled when she saw I'd eaten everything.

"You look a bit better now," she said. "Stay in bed mind, until it wears off."

I wanted her to stay and talk to me. But she loaded the pots onto her trolley and I was left in limbo once again.

It was still light, but I was convinced it was getting towards evening when I heard the voices again, more clearly now, and getting nearer. My whole body prickled with apprehension. Was there more trouble ahead? I lay back on my pillow, my fists clenched, determined to defend myself, but at the same time not at all sure I was strong enough. When the door opened, it was a little like a mirage. A sea of friendly faces; laughing, bickering and chattering.

"Look!" shouted one, pointing at my bed.

A pretty girl, with black skin and long dark hair, bounded over.

"I'm Sandy," she announced, her whole face open and friendly. And, more softly: "What's your name? Are you OK, duck?"

Her tenderness was so unexpected that it shocked me, and I felt tears of emotion pricking at my eyes.

"Carol," I mumbled.

"Bet you're wondering what's going on," said Sandy, perching on the cupboard at the side of my bed. "You've been in the treatment room, haven't you?"

I nodded, painfully aware of the sticky sensation between my legs. My limbs still felt leaden, as though they didn't belong to me, even after a whole day's rest. I wanted to ask Sandy if she'd suffered too and if she'd met Dr Milner. But saying it out loud would somehow make it real and acknowledge that it had happened. And I wasn't ready for that. Sandy chatted away, introducing the girls around her. I even recognised a few of the faces, Tania, Dolly and Sara, because they lived near to me in Derby.

"What the bloody hell are you doing in here?" gasped Tania, when she spotted me.

I shrugged.

"Don't know," I said honestly. "I ran away. That's it, I suppose. But I'm not ill, I've nothing wrong with me. I don't know why I'm in hospital."

"I've no idea why I'm here," Sandy told me, equally perplexed. "I'm not ill."

"Me neither," piped up another voice. "Me neither," said another.

Sara, I knew, was from a lovely home. She had good parents, nothing like mine. None of this made any sense. I'd been here over a day, and I still didn't even know what Aston Hall was.

"Aston Hall is a psychiatric hospital," Sandy explained. "But it's more like a prison, Carol. There are locks on the doors and windows. You can't get out. You're stuck."

She smiled kindly, to ease the blow.

"Stuck here with us, babs," she repeated.

Her words should have struck fear through me. But she spoke with such warmth and gentleness that I felt a sense of relief. Even in those first few moments, I felt a connection with Sandy, and I knew we were going to be firm friends. For a long time, I had felt so incredibly and painfully lonely. Now I was no longer on my own.

*****

The entire ward was filled with teenage girls, around my age, but there was one old lady, Doris, who slept in an end bed. She had a black and white dog, Rex, and he slept on a blanket on the floor at her side.

"She's the Nurses' Nark," whispered Sandy, as the girls

all changed into their nightdresses. "She's so bad tempered. Watch out for her."

Doris was around 70 years of age, I was surprised to see her on a ward with young girls and even more taken-aback that she was allowed to keep a dog. Rex seemed so incongruous in those sterile surroundings.

"The dog's lovely," Sandy said. "Don't worry about him. It's Doris you should be scared of."

As luck would have it, my bed was next to Sandy's and we chatted until late at night. My eyelids were still heavy after the sedation, but I was eager to learn everything I could about Aston Hall. Every so often, the night nurse would pop her head in the ward to check we were all asleep. But we could hear her heels on the parquet floor, advertising her arrival, so she didn't once catch us out. We simply closed our eyes and lay still, the moment we heard the tap-tap of her shoes and then waited until they faded into the distance, before we started chatting again.

"Phew, that was close," I giggled, when it was safe to open my eyes again. "I was desperate to cough when she was in here just then."

Sandy laughed.

"You'll get used to it," she replied. "I've had the pillow in my mouth before now to stop me making a noise."

Sandy was a few months younger than me, but she revealed she had already been in Aston Hall for almost two years.

"Two years!" I gasped. "Oh, that's awful. Why can't you go home?"

Sandy shook her head.

"Don't know," she said. "Don't really know why I'm here and why I can't go home. Mind you, I don't want to go home. But I don't want to be in here, either. I'm sort of stuck."

In a low voice, Sandy confided that she had been through a horrific ordeal at home. Afterwards, she had been taken to the Cedars and then to Aston Hall. Most of the girls on the ward had been through some form of abuse. Some were from families who'd had too many children and simply couldn't cope. Others had been abandoned by their parents. Through the darkness, Sandy pointed out each bed one by one, and attached to each young face was a story of despair and inhumanity. Every young girl had been failed so tragically, then plucked like carrion from their home by vultures dressed as social workers. It was so cruel.

"What about you, Carol?" asked Sandy. "What's your story?"

I sucked in my breath. I had kept this to myself for so long, but now I could unburden myself and I knew, absolutely, as with Catherine, that Sandy would believe me. This time however, unlike Catherine, Sandy understood. Sandy had a bond with me, almost as though she could see right through to my soul. And once I began speaking, the words tumbled out, one after another, as if they had been anxious to escape.

"My brother sexually abused me," I said, in a hushed voice. "He forced me to give him oral sex. He used kitchen cutlery, time after time, year after year. I told my mum, but she didn't believe me. I told the social worker, but she didn't believe me either.

"I kind of gave up after that. I thought nobody was bothered."

Again, it should have left me feeling distraught, reliving my ordeal in such graphic detail. But actually, I felt a strange sense of relief, almost as if some of the unbearable weight had been lifted from me. We had all suffered – we were all suffering still – but at Aston Hall, we were in it together.

I was, according to my social worker, dysfunctional and damaged. But here, I felt I had found kindred spirits. I felt buoyed and supported. I might not belong in Aston Hall, but I certainly belonged with these girls. I remembered how, as a little girl, I had loved exploring the grounds of the hospital behind our house, and how I had terrified myself with what might lie behind the walls of institutions like that. Well, I was about to find out. I was on the other side of those walls now.

As I drifted off to sleep, I tried to block out the memory of Milner and the treatment room and focus instead on my new-found friends.

Chapter Ten

*****

The following morning, at 6am, we were all awoken by a nurse.

"Come on, downstairs," yawned Sandy. "Time for a shower."

In a line, we made our way down the concrete stairs, all the way to the basement, where we waited our turn for either a bath or a shower. A nurse handed me a towel and soap, and another one gave me a bundle of clothes.

The basement itself was gloomy and dimly lit and a shiver ran down my spine as I stood in line. Despite the chatter of the girls, like early morning birds, it was a spooky place, made worse by the steam hissing from the shower cubicles. The large water pipes which ran along the walls gargled and grumbled as the Victorian plumbing system was stretched to the limit. It sounded as though there was a monster trapped inside, hammering to get out. But I knew better than that. I knew the monster was already here, wearing a grey suit and a pair of glasses.

After we were showered and dressed, it was back to the ward to make our beds under the watchful eye of Nurse Clackton.

"Hospital corners," she reminded us. "There can be no beauty without neatness and order."

I had no idea what hospital corners were. Sandy showed me, hurriedly, whilst trying to do her own bed too.

"Any untidy beds will be punished," rapped Nurse Clackton, as she strode up and down the ward, ready to lash us with an imaginary whip.

"Not good enough," she shouted suddenly, stopping at one bed.

The poor girl was ordered to scrub the concrete steps outside the ward – and miss her breakfast. I was indignant, but the other girls barely reacted. They went about their chores quietly, passively almost. After the beds were inspected, we filed downstairs to a large hall, the same size as the ward. There, I helped to put up trestle tables and chairs, ready for breakfast. The food arrived from the kitchen, which was in another building in the complex. My heart sank when I saw trays of grapefruit. I remembered my disastrous trip to Skegness.

"What, no sugar?" I asked. "I can't eat that, it's too sour. I've tried it before."

But the other girls, again, simply did as they were instructed. And I remembered the poor girl who was scrubbing the concrete steps and decided I should keep my mouth shut and do as I was told.

Afterwards, we were given cereal and tea, and I ate as much as I wanted. This was a new experience for me – having food and lots of it, all prepared by someone else. I felt refreshed and more positive as I drained my mug.

"That was lovely," I said to Sandy.

Next, we were split into groups; some girls did the

washing up, others helped put the tables away. I was instructed to count all the plates, dishes and cutlery, in case any had been stolen. As I counted the knives, forks and spoons, and laid them in neat piles, I was suddenly back on the bunk bed, with Ian holding me down, his mouth hanging open in an inane grin, and spots of saliva landing on my face. I shook myself out of it, but dropped the spoons in the drawer as though they were burning hot.

"All done here," I said. "So what happens now?"

"Nothing," Sandy replied dully. "Nothing at all."

With the furniture all tidied away to the side, we all stood in the empty hall, arms hanging loosely. There were no games, no distractions. There was a TV which was switched off, but there was no radio. Unless I was at Aunty Bet's, I didn't really like playing pop music, because it reminded me of Ian. But this was the late 60s, and many of the girls wanted to dance and sing. We were part of a generation that was enjoying new freedoms and breaking down boundaries. Yet here we were, locked up; emotional, physical and sexual prisoners. The irony was grotesque. And apart from one chair, which was reserved for Doris, we didn't even have anywhere to sit down. There were no cushions, not even a rug. Sandy and I sat on the hard floor, along with Tania.

"How do you feel after the treatment room?" Tania asked me.

She must have seen me squirm, because she added:

"Don't worry, everyone gets it. He picks a different girl every time he comes. You get a dose of the truth drug and then he knocks you out and does whatever he likes. Does that sound familiar?"

I nodded uneasily, the memory of my sticky inner thighs and the stinging sensation suddenly brought into sharp focus again. I realised how foolish I had been, looking forward to 'the truth drug' as some form of solution. Really, it was just another way of keeping me quiet.

"It's rape, you know," Tania said quietly. "He does it when you're unconscious. Dirty bastard."

I stared at her, appalled. I knew what rape was. But I'd never had sexual intercourse with anyone. My only sexual experience had been a forced one, by my own brother. It hadn't occurred to me that Milner had gone even further. When I'd heard the rattle of instruments on his tray, I had naively presumed he had done the same to me as Ian did. But some of the girls were far more worldly than me and they had been sexually active before they came into Aston Hall. They recognised the signs.

"Oh, it's rape alright," said Tania miserably. "Either that or sexual assault. You can never be sure which one he goes for, because you're never awake."

I couldn't believe how cursed I was. I had run away from home to escape my brother's abuse and run straight into the lion's den. I even wondered if there was a connection between my brother and Milner. It seemed unfathomable that I could be abused by two different people who, as far as I knew, had never even met. Back then, I had no idea that the first period of abuse had facilitated the second. Milner had pounced precisely because he knew I was vulnerable. He knew I was broken. And, under the pretence of putting me back together, he would simply break me even further.

Even Sandy, who had been in there for two years, had no idea why Milner administered a truth drug and then fired the same questions, over and over, at his victim. It seemed we were part of some macabre experiment; trapped in a real-life horror film.

Mid-morning, Nurse Clackton began calling us, one by one, into her office. If nothing else, it was something new to focus on.

"It's medication time," Sandy whispered. "Don't argue, it's not worth it. Just take what they give you."

I trusted Sandy and so, when I heard my name: "Mackie!" I did as she said. But when Nurse Clackton tipped a handful of pills straight into my mouth, I battled against it. Again, I wanted to scream out that I wasn't ill. I didn't need to be in hospital. I certainly didn't need drugs.

As I walked back to the ward I stumbled, I felt woozy and disorientated. All around me, girls were slumping on the floor, some moaning, some grinding their teeth. One by one, we were zonking out. It was so warm too, a sickly, hospital warmth.

I felt as though my spirit was being sucked out, through

my mouth, and into the atmosphere. I had no fight left, no bones even, as I sank to the floor like a crumpled heap of clothes.

All day, I seemed to doze, in and out of sleep. There was a hospital cat – locked indoors just like us – and it padded quietly up and down the hallway, or slept in the corners alongside the girls. I wondered if the cat was drugged up, too. Sometimes, I wondered if the animal even existed, or if it was a figment of my starved and fractured imagination.

"You'll get used to it," Sandy reassured me, her head lolling against mine. "They medicate us to keep us quiet. But you'll be able to stay awake, if you concentrate."

Now I understood the passivity, the desultory acceptance of the girls. Their personalities, their very beings, were being diluted and washed away by medicine.

"What's in the medicine?" I asked Sandy.

"I think it's called Largactil," she replied. "You watch, you'll be doing the 'Largactil shuffle' before too long."

I giggled. It sounded like a sort of dance.

"It's where you can't pick your feet up properly," Sandy explained. "It happens to everyone."

Even without the drugs, I imagined Sandy was usually a placid and a kind-hearted girl. She had more humanity, and had showed me more affection, than anyone I had ever met. As the afternoon wore on, the girls tried, in their own ways, to stimulate themselves. It was hard to tell whether it was boredom or medication that was slowing us down, or a combination of the two. Some girls ground their teeth. Others pulled out clumps of their hair, which made me wince as I watched. And a few rocked quietly, back and forth, as though they could hear imaginary music.

"That won't happen to me," I said to myself firmly. "That can't happen. I won't let it."

At 5pm it was time to get the tables and chairs out again and we were given a lovely meal of steak pie and mashed potato. Even though I was sedated, I was also terribly bored, and so I ate, just for something to do. I had to admit, too, the food here was much nicer than anything I'd ever had at home.

"You make sure you clean your plate, Mackie," said Clackton, her breath on my shoulder. "You're underweight, according to my chart. We need to feed you up. I'll have you on the scales every week and I want to see some progress."

For a horrible moment, I had the idea that Dr Milner was feeding me up so that he could eat me, like a Christmas turkey. I imagined him coming into the treatment room and getting out a knife and fork. But instead of sexually assaulting me, as Ian had, he would simply tuck in and carve me into pieces.

"Mmm, lovely slice of thigh, Mackie… Do pass the brown sauce, Sister Clackton."

The image made me shudder, and when afters arrived – a jam pudding with custard – I couldn't face it. To me, the jam looked like congealed blood and I convinced myself it could be human. Instead, I fed titbits to Rex, who was waiting underneath the table for scraps. His wet nose in my palm reminded me of my own dog, Peter, and I felt a twinge of homesickness. I hoped someone was feeding him and taking him for walks. I wondered how the little ones were getting along. And I wondered if anyone had missed me. Anyone at all.

That evening, after the meal was finished and tidied away, we were allowed to watch TV. But Doris had planted her chair firmly in front of the screen, meaning the rest of us could hardly see it. And she had complete control over the programme choice, too. Doris liked watching *Coronation Street* and nature programmes. Nobody else was allowed to have a say.

"I'd love to watch *Top of the Pops*, just once," Sandy said wistfully.

I felt enraged on Sandy's behalf. She was full of goodness. Was it too much to ask for her to watch just one programme, once a week? I wanted some of the other girls to complain and object, too, but they were quiet and jaded, heads hanging heavy, either through boredom or medication in weary compliance. So it was down to me. Sandy had been a good friend to me so far and I wanted to repay her.

"Why can't the girls have a choice sometimes?" I asked Doris, my hands on my hips. I wanted her to see I meant business.

She turned to me and said: "I've been in this place for over 30 years. I decide what we watch."

"That's not fair," I said, but she had already turned back to the TV.

Complaining bitterly to myself, I went to sit back on the floor with Sandy. When the soap operas were finished, Doris called me over.

"You're new, aren't you?" she said. "Why are you in here?"

I clammed up.

"Go on," she pressed. "Answer the question."

"Not saying," I said flatly.

"I'm a lot older than you, I can help you," she said. "Tell me what went wrong."

But I didn't trust her one bit. Besides, I didn't need a mother figure. I had one mother already and that had not worked out well at all, so I was hardly likely to want a second one.

"I'm fine," I replied shortly. "Really, I don't need your help."

My resentment towards Doris grew sharper. I reasoned that she could have helped us, shown us the tricks of survival if she wanted to. She had managed 30 years in there, so surely she had learned some short-cuts. But she only wanted to hear our stories, she never shared her own. I suspected, even back then, that she might be a spy, working for Milner and Clackton. I resolved to have nothing to do with her. Now, with the wisdom of hindsight, I believe she was more likely wholly institutionalised and had probably forgotten how to talk about herself, and how to make friends, whether or not she wanted to.

In bed that night, Sandy and I chatted again until we heard the tell-tale tap-tap warning of Nurse Clackton's shoes.

"Clack by name, Clack-Clack by nature," I giggled, and we hid our faces in our pillows, to muffle our laughter.

When the ward doors swung open, I heard Doris' voice, clear and unmistakeable cut through the silence.

"Sandy and Carol have been talking and keeping us all awake," she said peevishly. "I wish they'd go to sleep."

Nurse Clackton marched over to our beds and I could feel her spraying saliva on my cheek.

"You will both scrub the steps tomorrow," she said. "And then maybe you will learn what it is to be obedient."

Chapter Eleven

The next morning, before the showers, there was a mad scramble down to the laundry to get the best clothes. We were each given one pair of shoes but, as at The Cedars, none of the girls were allowed to own their own clothes and instead, we each grabbed whatever we could from a huge pile of mish-mash dresses, cardigans, socks, and knickers.

My clothes the day before hadn't even fit me; the dress hung from me like a tent and I'd had to knot the knickers to stop them from falling down. So I was keen, like everyone else, to be first in the queue. There was a scrum outside the laundry and some of the girls were squabbling and squawking like angry starlings.

"It's usually the Derby girls against the outsiders," Sandy told me with a wry smile. "All hot air and nothing to worry about."

Unlike Sandy, I'd happily have dived in and scrapped for the best pair of knickers. I had no qualms about that. But she had such grace and dignity and it left me wishing I could be more like her. Even our punishment, scrubbing steps on our hands and knees, was not so bad, side by side. I loved having a true friend. I appreciated having a confidante. We were so different, yet we complemented each other perfectly. I knew there were tough times ahead, but I also felt I could cope, with Sandy by my side.

The following morning, as we all waited for breakfast outside the hall, one of the girls, nearest to the window, exclaimed:

"There's his car outside! He's here. Someone's getting it today."

There was a sharp and collective intake of breath which seemed to run through the line of girls like an electric shock.

"Who's here?" I hissed to Sandy. "Whose car is it?"

"Milner," she whispered. "He's here to choose a girl. We'll find out who it is because they won't be allowed breakfast. You can't have breakfast if you're having the jab."

I felt heavy with dread, as though I was carrying a stomach full of sludge. And when I sat down at the breakfast table, Nurse Clackton pointed at me and said: "No breakfast, Mackie."

That was all it took. It was enough for every pair of eyes to turn on mine, their expressions a peculiar mix of relief and sympathy. They were sorry it was me, but gladder still that it wasn't them.

"You'll be fine," Tania whispered, squeezing my hand. "You'll get through it."

Chapter Eleven

But this time, I knew what was coming. And that made it much more difficult. The anticipation was almost worse than the abuse itself.

Clackton took me out of the hall, back upstairs and through the large, locked door of the treatment room. It was chilly in there, cold even, despite the bright skies outside and the promise of a sunny day ahead. Once again, I was made to strip, strapped into the jacket and bound by my hands and feet. I was alone for a couple of hours, waiting as if for the gallows.

As I lay on the mattress I wished, more than anything, that I could float away, that I could somehow smash through the barriers of time and place and escape to a new dimension. For what alternative could be worse than this? If I squeezed my eyes and wished, really wished, perhaps I could make it happen?

"Well, Mackie, have we been a good girl?" asked Milner smoothly as the door opened.

He took the syringe and drew it back, and my blood ran icy cold. Again, I had the sensation that I was being paralysed from the neck down. I had that same woozy feeling, slightly sickly, slightly sleepy. Yet it was relaxing, too. I couldn't work out how I could be comforted yet terrorised at the same time.

"Tell me why you ran away," Milner began. "Tell me what happened at home."

Despite myself, I sighed with impatience.

"I have told you the answers already," I said. "You don't believe me. You're the same as the rest of them."

"Tell me why you ran away," he repeated.

"How come you ask the questions and not me?" I complained.

In reply, Milner refilled his syringe and injected me once again. This time, I felt a rush of nausea. My lesson learnt, I answered his questions, all the same as last time, all with the same answers.

"My brother abuses me. I ran away. Nobody listened…"

When I was finished, I felt a quick flash of sheer terror as he dropped the gauze over my face, and I was knocked unconscious. It was dark when I awoke and the drugged-up, hungover feeling was by now familiar to me, but no less frightening. Thankfully, there was no pain or bleeding down below. I had escaped that, at least. For the rest of the night I floated in and out of consciousness, at times shivering with cold, at others drenched with sweat.

After it grew light, Nurse Clackton took me back to the empty ward, all the girls having gone for breakfast. Just as before, I spent the day in bed, waiting for my friends to return later.

"Did you have it? The jab?" they asked, clamouring around my bed like moths.

I nodded wearily.

"Yes," I murmured. "Hope that's my turn over with now. Twice in a week."

Sandy shook her head as she got into her bed beside me.

"That's not how it works," she said. "Sometimes he chooses the same girl three times on the trot. Other times, we don't see him for months."

I soon learned that she was right. There was no pattern to Milner's abuse. And the unpredictability made it all the more hideous. Sometimes, as we were setting up the tables and chairs for breakfast, we caught his voice from the office, and it was like a wicked spell had been cast. The girls all froze, as if turned to stone. Then came Clackton's voice, loud and commanding:

"Jones!" she yelled. "Jones to the office. No breakfast for Jones!"

In terror, we all ran to hide behind the long, floor length curtains which hung at every window. Breathing hard behind the musty smelling material we hoped, desperately, that we could simply melt away. Like little children, we believed if we couldn't see Clackton, she couldn't see us. But her voice just became louder, and angrier:

"Jones! Now!"

One girl, so terrified when her name was called, wet herself right there and then. Seemingly unaware of the puddle at her feet, she begged and pleaded and sobbed to be spared. But as much as I felt sorry for her, I was, more than anything, pleased that it was her, and not me. I had a reprieve, if just for today. It could have been divisive, this pick and mix of little lambs to the slaughter. But in fact, the cruel method of selection only pushed us closer together. There was a camaraderie in our collective hardship, a solace in our joint suffering. We always made a fuss of the girl who was chosen. We made sure she knew she was not alone. And that was all we could do. We even made up a song about Milner, which we sang loudly on the ward:

"Milner, Milner, he's so bad. He's much worse than your bloody dad."

To me, it was just a neat rhyme. Looking back now, I realise some of the girls were in Aston Hall because they had been abused by their fathers. And so now, the song is not as funny as I had once thought.

*****

The weeks rolled into months and every day, every single, wretched day, was exactly the same. There was a weekly menu, which, if nothing else, helped us to remember what day it was.

"Shepherd's pie, must be Tuesday," I reminded myself. "Rhubarb crumble, so it's Friday."

I loved the food at Aston Hall. In comparison with the meagre portions and the crisp butties at home, this was tasty and nutritional. My favourite was the roast dinners and the sponge cakes. I loved the rice pudding, too, but it came with a thick skin on top which I hated. It was a challenge to scrape off the skin and feed it either to the cat or to Rex the dog, without being spotted by Clackton. I had weekly weigh-in sessions, which showed I was slowly gaining weight and becoming healthier.

Milner's warped abuse of the girls on the ward continued. Always with the same pattern, always with the same questions. It felt like we were stuck on rewind and repeat – playing the same section of our lives, over and over, on a loop. We were small, insignificant ants, trapped on a monster's merry-go-round. There was no way off and no way out.

Milner often stayed at the Mansion House, in the hospital grounds. And some mornings, maybe twice a week, maybe less often, he would stroll into the ward to pick out a new plaything. We were no more than chunks of sacrificial meat, offered up to the treatment room altar, for Milner to feast upon.

It was impossible to get used to what he was doing, this was never something I could simply brush aside. And yet, as time went on, I became passive and compliant. My once feisty nature was chiselled away, piece by piece, until I was flattened out; identical to everyone around me. I was losing my sense of self. Perhaps it was a survival instinct, knowing that acceptance was the only way. And the drugs surely played their part too. I was so heavily sedated for so much of the time, that I barely had the energy to hold up my head, never mind stand up to Milner. I found myself shuffling from my bed, to the bathroom, to the hall, and back to bed.

Sandy was right. The shuffle had got me, just as she had predicted.

But in other ways, I became much harder and tougher. I blocked my family out of my mind, refusing to allow myself to think of my younger siblings. I couldn't afford to become weak and sentimental, not with predators like Clackton circling around me, ready to zap me with another drug as soon as I showed signs of cracking.

The other girls had warned me that we were not allowed visitors, and of course I had no expectation at all that my mother might make contact. But a small part of me, in those first few months, hoped against hope that my father, or perhaps Aunt Bet, or even my Scottish grandparents, would wonder where I was. Why didn't they come to see me, or even send me a letter? Surely Aunt Bet would want to know I was safe? I had the feeling she wouldn't stand for Milner's behaviour. Yet there was nothing. Was I so worthless, so easily disposed of, that I was not even worth a phone call?

I imagined Margaret at home, busy with the little ones, usurping my role. Had they all simply forgotten about me? I remembered my sisters outside the window at the Cedars, shouting my name. Every time I looked at my finger – and saw the missing tip – I remembered that day, and I could see in my mind's eye their faces shining with mischief and excitement as they were chased away by Miss Halliwell. How could it be that they had wiped me from their lives so quickly and so efficiently? Again, I could not allow myself to be overwhelmed by grief or self-pity. To ride this out, I had to be strong and hold firm. Over time, my emotions became set like granite. It was the only way.

One Monday morning, we heard a new girl arriving in the office and, as I watched her, trembling next to her social worker, I could see myself, right there, in her place. My heart went out to her – and yet – I would not, could not, soften towards her. I ought to have offered her comfort and support. Instead, to my shame, I and a few of the other girls scurried to the office door and chanted:

"You're getting the jab! You're getting the jab!"

It was ruthless. Horribly cruel. But being mean to her made us feel better, just for a few moments. We were desensitised and institutionalised. Yes, our hardship did bring us closer together, most of the time. But there were times when it ripped us apart and we were nasty to each other. We were just kids, after all. Ours was a real-life, real-pain *Lord of the Flies* – right here, in Derby.

Afterwards, I felt so wretched and disgusted with myself that I vowed to make it up to her, as soon as she came out of the treatment room.

"I'm Carol," I smiled. "You can borrow my soap and toothpaste if you haven't got any. And I'll show you round as well."

I tried to be friendly, but I could not afford to let my guard down completely, just as I could not allow myself to dwell on my memories of my siblings. I was worried I might crumble completely otherwise.

Occasionally, in my dreams, I would catch glimpses of little Lena or baby Alice, and I would wake with my pillow sodden with tears. I remembered our games of snakes and ladders, where I'd always let the younger ones win. But I remembered also my flares of temper and frustration. I wished, how I wished, that I had been calmer and more patient. But I could not have known what lay ahead. I could not have predicted that our time together would run out. Like little wooden dolls, I compartmentalised my siblings, putting them away in a box in my mind, hoping that one day, we would open it again together.

Chapter Twelve

One morning, I managed to make it to the breakfast table – and I was just about to have my first sip of tea – when I felt someone hovering behind me, like a black cloud.

"It's Clacko," whispered Sandy, her lips hardly moving.

"Late decision, you're wanted in the office Mackie," said Nurse Clackton. "No breakfast. Quick about it."

My whole body sagged with disappointment, and then in the next moment I was electrified with fear. Normally, Milner chose his prey before breakfast. I had got this far through the routine and believed that I was safe for the day. It seemed so cruel to spring it on me at such a late stage, especially when my stomach was empty and I could smell my breakfast on its way. My stomach growled in protest but I knew it was useless to object. Meekly, I followed Clackton back up the stairs, into the treatment room, and into Derby's very own version of purgatory. When Milner arrived, he gave me the same injection, and asked the same questions, and then – I imagined – performed the same sickening ritual of sexual abuse. The torment, whilst horrific and terrifying, was also strangely boring in its repetition and routine. I dreaded it. But I was sick of it, too, much in the same way that I got sick of scrubbing floors or counting cutlery.

"Tell me again why you ran away, Mackie..?"

'You know it's not good to tell lies, Mackie..."

'Tell me, Mackie, what was wrong at home..?"

I knew that insubordination would lead only to a second injection. But sometimes, I just couldn't hold back.

"Why do you accuse me of telling lies when you've given me a truth drug?" I asked. "Surely that means your drug isn't working very well?"

Milner didn't ever gratify my questions with a response. Instead, he simply refilled his syringe and I had just enough time to regret my impertinence before another wave of nausea overtook me. But later, in the ward, I would regale the other girls with exaggerated tales of my audacity, and it felt good to see them all laughing.

"You said what, Carol?!" gasped Sandy. "Oh, you're so cheeky. You really are."

But she giggled along with the others, and it warmed my heart that I had given them all a reason to smile.

Soon after, not that I minded, I was upstaged by another girl, Maureen. Her name was called out, early one morning, and at first, she refused to leave the sanctity of her hiding place behind the curtains.

"Not coming," she yelled.

By the time Clackton grabbed hold of her, Maureen's temper was simmering.

"I don't want to go," Maureen protested. "I hate the dirty bastard!"

Sandy sucked in her breath and shook her head.

"There will be trouble today," she said.

We didn't see Maureen for the rest of the day. But the next night, when we went up to the ward, she was waiting for us in bed, her eyes shining with mischief and triumph.

"Well?" I demanded. "How did it go?"

"I knocked his glasses off," Maureen announced proudly. "I did. He was in there, when Wacko Clacko was tying me up, lecturing me on how to behave. *'You really should control your temper, blah, blah, blah...'* So just as she was about to tie me up, I lashed out and knocked Milner's glasses flying. I managed to crack 'em I think. I gave him a right belt."

There was a mass murmur of approval amongst the girls.

"What did he do then?" I asked. "Was he mad at you? Did he hit you back?"

Maureen shook her head.

"No, I just got an extra dose of the drug," she said, her shoulders slumping at the memory. "And judging by how I feel... Well. Let's just say I've been punished."

The smiles left our faces in one broad sweep – as though our faces had been cleaned by a giant etch-a-sketch. No matter how we tried, there was no way of getting one over on Milner. He held all the cards, all the status, all the power.

*****

For many of us, strange as it might sound, the boredom was as big an issue as the abuse. Milner might pick out the same girl twice in one week, but then spare her for six months. It was impossible to anticipate or to prepare for the nightmare of the treatment room. And so it did not figure in my thoughts so much as you might think – unless it happened to be my turn.

Day after apathetic day, I paced the big hall, like a caged animal. All around me, girls mumbled and hummed and ground their teeth. One girl pulled her hair out in handfuls, leaving a small, pink, bald patch on the side of her head. I couldn't bear to look at it. It seemed to symbolise everything that was wrong with this place. Three of the girls had formed a lesbian love triangle and were locked in constant arguments, each chasing the others around the hall. These were all forms of occupation, all ways of escape. Clackton kept us all under surveillance. She allowed the behaviour to go only so far before she doled out punishments.

"You'll to go Rowan Ward if you carry on like this," she warned.

Rowan Ward was, we knew, for girls with severe psychiatric problems.

Chapter Twelve

I was determined not to be dragged under by the lethargy. But by the start of 1970, almost a year after my arrival, it became irresistible. One dreary afternoon, I let myself sink to the floor in the hall, and rocked myself gently, to and fro, to and fro, to and fro. The rhythm was so soothing. I closed my eyes and I allowed myself to remember the feeling of Ava's hand in mine as we walked to school. I could feel Peter's fur, rubbing against my face. I heard the twins squabbling over toys. It was such a comfort, just to rock myself. It was almost like a little window into my old life.

"Don't do it, Carol," said Sandy, gently, at my side. "It's not good for you."

I knew she was right. But it was like fighting an addiction, resisting the urge to rock myself. Instead, I began pacing the room, my head bobbing and nodding neurotically, peering at the large sash windows which looked out onto the grounds. Onto freedom. Each one was locked shut with a wooden block, screwed firmly into place. But I was determined – desperate – to find a way out. My imprisonment weighed me down, so much that I felt crushed, suffocated. The ward was big and airy and yet there were times I felt I could barely breathe. Even on sunny days, we weren't allowed so much as a breath of fresh air. We never left the ward. Not ever. So, if I was going to escape, I would have to make a break for it through one of the windows. It was the only way. I spent my days marching up and down, forensically examining each pane of glass for signs of weakness.

"Not that window, that won't do," I muttered to myself, moving on to the next one. "And not that one. And not that one, either."

My determination slowly gave way to frustration and I began pulling at my fingers, one by one.

"I need to get out of here!" I shouted suddenly. "I need to get out!"

Tania jumped to her feet, seizing on the diversion.

"Me too," she yelled.

The atmosphere was suddenly febrile, charged. It was like waiting for an electric storm. Three more girls gathered around us, an agitated coven, intent on trouble.

"What next?" asked one.

Before I could reply, one of the girls kicked out at a stack of tables, and it crashed to the floor. It was a domino effect. We ran riot, pulling at the curtains, kicking at tables and chairs, screaming at the tops of our voices. It was fantastic! Just hearing my own voice and making myself heard.

"Please, stop," Sandy pleaded. "You'll get into bother."

But we were too far gone. I felt fabulous, more alive and more present than I had for months. Tania tried scaling the curtains, to get to the window.

"I want to get out!" she screeched. "I've had enough."

Clackton and another nurse came dashing out of the office, bawling loudly.

"Calm down!" ordered Clackton. "Stop this nonsense now!"

"Piss off you old cow!" retorted one of the girls.

Clackton looked like she might combust with fury. She and the second nurse came for each of us, one by one, and dragged us off to the office. When it was my turn, I dug my heels in so that they squeaked along the wooden floor. I was like a little dog refusing to go for a walk, choking on my own lead. The irony was that a dog's life would actually have been far better than ours. At least we'd have been allowed outside every now and then for a walk.

In the office, I was given another dose of sedative and slowly, the fight leaked out of me. My blood seemed to run more slowly and sluggishly, through my veins, until it felt like lumpy custard. I was back to being a zombie.

"Right, you lot, Rowan Ward," Clackton announced.

Inwardly, I groaned. I knew Rowan Ward was for the mentally disturbed. We were lined up and taken outside. The ward was just a short walk away, in a nearby building. But just the feeling of the cold air on my face and the wind in my hair was lovely. It was so refreshing, a reminder that I was still breathing after all. We even walked past a bus stop, planted bizarrely at the end of a patch of grass. There was no road next to it and certainly no buses ever came this way.

"I bet Clackton put that bus stop there," I whispered to Tania. "All the runaways will stand there, waiting for a bus that never comes, and then she'll catch them. It's not a bus stop at all, It's a fishing net."

We walked into the new ward and it was a shock, an assault on our senses. A pungent stench of urine and faeces, and girls wailing and screeching. In the middle of the room there was a tangle of arms and legs belonging, I presumed, to patients, some only half-dressed.

"Give us a kiss," simpered one girl, heading towards me.

Uncertainly, I offered her my cheek, and she drew nearer with a smile. But in the next moment, I sprang back and yelped in pain.

"She bit me!" I shouted. "Ow! She bit me!"

The girl didn't flinch, she didn't even make eye contact. I was left, holding my face, gasping in shock, as she shuffled on to the next victim, repeating her mantra:

"Give us a kiss, give us a kiss."

Rowan Ward made Laburnum look like a civilised hotel and I wish I could say I was horrified. But the truth was, I was becoming numb to it all. I looked at the brown stains smeared across the walls, at the puddles of urine dotted all over the floor, and I simply picked my way through the mess. They didn't appal me in the way that they should have. There were girls slapping themselves around the head and body. Some were totally naked, strutting around the ward. Their behaviour was sexually inappropriate; it would cause uproar in the real world. Here, nobody batted an eyelid.

Chapter Twelve

"This is going to be fun," Tania muttered. "We'll go nuts in here."

We were shown to our beds by a nurse who was much kinder and friendlier than Clackton.

"You will be here for a week," she announced. "You must keep your wits about you, girls."

During the day, Tania and I stuck together and, shamefully, we found entertainment in the girls around us. We laughed hysterically at one girl who hit herself so hard she fell over. Another time, she hit someone else and a big fight broke out. Tania and I watched the brawl from a safe distance, and we loved every minute of it.

"Bet you tomorrow's pudding that the blonde one wins," Tania said to me.

"You're on," I replied.

After months staring at the same walls, rigid with lethargy, this was like a mini holiday. Never mind that these new walls were stained with faeces. Never mind that the girls around us were trying to bite us or show us their private parts. We giggled and sniggered, like it was all part of some crazy sideshow, all for our benefit.

Looking back, I wish, of course, that I had shown more compassion. But we were young girls, desperate and damaged ourselves, and we meant no harm. We couldn't beat the system, so we had joined it. What other option did we have?

Best of all, there was no sign of Milner that entire week.

He didn't seem to bother with the disabled children; the ones we asked had never even heard of him.

"We're on barley in here," Tania smiled. "I'd rather be in a ward like this than have the threat of Milner hanging over us."

So, if it was Clackton's intention to frighten us into behaving well, it backfired spectacularly. We were having a rather good time. The day before we were due to leave Rowan Ward, Tania said to me:

"I just can't go back to Laburnum. I can't face it, Carol."

"If you run away, you'll get caught," I told her. "It's not worth the risk."

"I'll take it," she replied.

I knew she was deadly serious.

That evening, as we washed up after the evening meal, I slipped a sharp knife into my pocket. It wasn't something I could have got away with on Laburnum. But the nurses on Rowan were too occupied looking after the other girls and so paid us very little attention.

"Knives and forks all counted, all present and correct," I announced to the nurse in charge.

She was too busy grappling with another patient to double-check and she took me at my word. Afterwards, we were allowed an hour in the hall before bed. The two nurses were distracted elsewhere, and the other patients didn't notice or recognise what we were doing. Breathing loudly, with my heart hammering against my chest, I took the knife out from my pocket. The block unscrewed more quickly than I'd expected, and in just a couple of minutes, the window swung open and the cold air hit my face. The smell of the outside was so inviting that I was almost tempted to jump out myself.

"Be careful," I whispered, as Tania climbed up onto the windowsill.

"Wait for me," said another voice at my shoulder.

It was Suzy, one of our lot from Laburnum.

One after the other they jumped out, onto the grass below, and began running. I heard Tania swear in protest as she scratched her leg on a bramble and my heart thumped even harder. Darkness was falling but I could just make out their shapes as they disappeared across the fields. I had a moment of unbearable envy where I wished, I so wished, it could be me, too. But it was quickly swamped by a feeling of anxiety, because I knew they would live to regret their dash for freedom.

Quietly, I closed the window and sidled back into the kitchen, to replace the knife. Nobody had noticed. It had all been so simple. It was only when we were lining up at bedtime that they were missed.

"Where's Tania, where's Suzy?" asked a nurse.

I shrugged.

"Bathroom?" I suggested.

I hoped I was a good liar. There was no panic at first – we filed upstairs, whilst the nurses checked the toilets. But by the time I was undressed and ready for bed, there was a full-scale search in progress. Nurse Clackton appeared on the ward, spitting with rage.

"What do you know about this?" she demanded, thundering towards me.

"Nothing," I replied innocently.

All night I lay awake, imagining Tania and Suzy sleeping in the woods or sheltering in an outbuilding. I hoped they were safe and warm. More than anything, I hoped they were still free.

"Good luck girls," I whispered.

The next morning, I was taken back to Laburnum Ward, along with the other remaining girls who had been punished alongside me. At breakfast, I looked for Sandy, and I was bursting with the news.

"Wow, have I got a lot to tell you," I whispered.

"I heard about Tania and Suzy," Sandy replied.

I tried to give her a wink as I swallowed a spoonful of sour grapefruit, but the taste made me screw my face up in disgust, and we both giggled.

"Let's hope they make it," Sandy smiled. "It was a crazy thing to do."

The longer we went without hearing anything, the more promising it sounded. But even as we were tidying away after breakfast, a shout went up from one of the girls.

"They're back," she announced. "There's Tania in the office. I can see Suzy as well."

My heart dropped like a stone. I'd known this would happen. But I had hoped against hope for a little miracle. And it was so soon, too. They hadn't even had 24 hours of freedom. We all rushed to the door of the hall and I craned my neck to see the two girls, heads bowed. From my position, I couldn't see their faces. But I could sense their fear. Part of me worried that they might tell Clackton about my involvement. After all, I was guilty, too, I'd stolen the escape knife. But I should have known better. Us girls were loyal to each other. We stuck together, no matter what.

Clackton marched out of the office later and walked straight past me. Clearly, they'd not mentioned my name and she had no idea I had helped them. I breathed a silent thank you.

Suzy was allowed back onto the ward later that day, but Tania was immediately transferred to another hospital. I had no idea where. I missed her terribly. Her rebellious streak and her sense of humour had kept me going through the tougher times. I vowed to myself that once I was free of this place, and free of this torture, I would find her again. At night, in bed, Sandy and I often talked about Tania, laughing about her fiery temper and the endless scrapes she got herself into.

"Where is she now?" I wondered.

We both dreaded the thought – one that neither of us dared voice – that she might not even be alive.

A few months after Tania's escape, we were woken early one morning, even before Clackton made her appearance, by the sound of police sirens outside.

"Look out here!" shouted one of the girls, dashing to the window. We all clamoured, in our night clothes, for a good view. Outside the windows was a line of bushes and brambles; beyond them, fields, and beyond the fields, the River Trent. In the distance, we could see a line of police officers, combing the riverbank.

"Someone's in the river," said Sandy, sadly. "It's happened before."

I stared at her in confusion.

"What do you mean? Swimming?" I asked.

"No," she replied. "It will be a runaway. Over the years there have been a few kids trying to cross the river to escape. They don't always make it."

A shiver ran right through me.

"Right girls, these beds won't make themselves!" barked Clackton behind us. "Come away from that window. Back to it!"

At breakfast, the talk was all about the runaway. We didn't know who it was or even if they had been found. There was nobody missing from Laburnum, we had all been counted and recounted.

"Might be one of the boys," I said. "Poor lad. At least it's not one of us."

Later that day, the news was confirmed. One of the

boys from another ward had tried to run away and had tragically drowned in the river. There were lurid rumours that he had walked, trance-like, into the river, driven by desperation and dazed by drugs. Others claimed that he had dived in to swim across and had misjudged the swirling current. We heard stories, too, that he had been buried in an unmarked grave in the hospital grounds, until his body was later moved at the request of his family to a cemetery. I had no idea how much of this was true.

Afterwards, as I lay in bed at night, I heard his voice, thin and mournful on the wind, as the glass rattled in the window frames. His drowning ghost invaded my dreams, his arms reaching out to me for help, as he was dragged under by the reeds. In the dark corners of the hospital, I saw his eyes, like two black holes, bottomless tunnels of despair. And when the hot water pipes groaned and bubbled in the basement bathrooms, I fancied I could hear his hopeless screams. I didn't know the boy. I never even knew his name. But I knew his death would live with me forever. Any ambitions I had to escape were dented by Tania's capture and then crushed completely with the death of the poor nameless, faceless, boy. I could not risk running away.

Instead, one morning after breakfast, I freed the hospital cat instead. The windows in the hall opened a few inches, just wide enough for me to squeeze the cat through. So, whilst nobody was looking, I scooped her up and plopped her gently onto the ground outside.

"Run away," I said softly. "Run as fast as you can. And don't ever look back."

I could not taste freedom or feel the fresh air on my face. But it gladdened me to know that the cat could do so on my behalf.

Chapter Thirteen

Late in the spring of 1970, a little over a year after my arrival at Aston Hall, one of the girls, on the morning look-out for Milner's car, suddenly shouted:

"There's a van outside. F. B. Atkins. Who's that then?"

The words sent an instant thrill through me. My dad worked for F. B. Atkins and he drove a works van. Surely this was no coincidence? I ran out of the breakfast queue over to the window and, sure enough, there was my dad, his care-worn face peering uncertainly through his driver's window, right at me. And next to him, on the passenger seat, was Peter. My Peter! My dog! I had vowed not to let this happen, but I was suddenly choked with emotion and joy. This could mean only one thing. My dad had come to take me home!

In my mind, I banged on the window as hard as I could and screamed his name and Peter's name so loudly it felt as though my lungs might burst. In reality, I was slow and sluggish with sedation, and I managed only feeble taps on the window, and my voice was thin and pitiful.

"Dad!" I managed weakly. "I'm here, I'm here."

And then, sharp nails dug into my shoulders and I was dragged backwards, away from the window and into the nurses' office. Outside of my wails, I was dimly aware of Sister Clackton marching outside, towards my father.

"If you don't leave, I will call the police!" she yelled.

In desolation, I watched as he turned the van around and drove slowly away from me, my one hope, my only glimmer of rescue, gone. My last memory was of Peter, hanging out of the window, his loyal face turned towards me, his ears flattened by the breeze.

In the days afterwards, I slumped in the corner of the hall, rocking back and forth, back and forth, back and forth, like a broken toy.

*****

Those days after Dad's visit felt so lonely. It was as if my insides had been scooped out, and I was left feeling completely empty and hollow. Despite myself, I spent hours standing at the window, scanning the driveway for Dad's van. I knew he wasn't coming, but I couldn't help myself. It was like picking a scab, knowing it would bleed.

"You're going to feel worse if you stand at that window all day," Sandy said gently.

"There's nothing else to do," I retorted grumpily.

I missed my dad, and my younger siblings, too. But

I had no desire to see my mother, and certainly not my abusive and bullying big brother. And so my thoughts of home were conflicted and confused.

"Sorry, Sandy," I said eventually. "I'm in a bad mood today. I'm just sick of this place."

She nodded and looped her arm through mine.

"I know the feeling, duck," she said. "It's miserable."

But that night, just when I needed it the most, something happened to cheer us all up immeasurably. Apart from Sister Clackton and Dr Milner, the staff at Aston Hall were generally decent towards us, some were even sympathetic. Then that evening, as we were getting undressed for bed, a new nurse appeared.

"I'm Nurse Grantham," she smiled. "I'll be doing the night shift here from now on."

She was much older than the other nurses and to me, as a teenager, she seemed ancient. But she was kindness and gentleness itself.

"You girls shouldn't be locked up in here like this," she said sadly. "I don't like it."

She let us chatter and giggle until it was late. The next night, she brought biscuits, and we all had a snack before bed.

"Who fancies a bourbon?" she asked, handing round a biscuit tin.

I couldn't believe my luck. And then one night, she produced a packet of cigarettes.

"Who smokes?" she asked, with a cheeky grin.

I had never had a cigarette in my life, but I wasn't about to pass up the opportunity to rebel. The first couple of drags almost choked me, but then I got used to it. I held my cigarette out at a jaunty angle and pretended to be a rock star.

"All we need now is a bottle of cider," I joked.

From then on, Nurse Grantham would often bring in a packet of cigarettes, and lay them on the floor at the end of the ward, next to a large ashtray. By the morning, all the evidence was cleared away, and the place smelled of bleach once again. Nobody would have suspected a thing. She was like the Mary Poppins of the nursing community. I always worried that Doris would report us to Sister Clackton, she was just a few feet away in bed whilst we were enjoying our midnight feasts and our smokes. Doris was, after all, the Nurses' Nark and so far she had lived up to her reputation. One night, she overheard me telling a joke to the other girls.

"How does the Man in the Moon cut his hair?" I asked.

"No idea, Carol," they all shrugged.

"Eclipse it!" I yelled, throwing my hands in the air.

We all burst out laughing, not because it was particularly funny, but because we would have laughed at virtually anything. We were young girls, looking for lightness and relief, determined to make the best of our strange situation. But later, when Sister Clackton poked her head into the ward to check on us, Doris piped up:

"Carol Mackie has been distracting the girls with jokes. She's disturbing us all."

Sister Clackton marched over to my bed and, though I squeezed my eyes closed, I knew it was no use.

"You will be appropriately punished for this," she snarled, and then she left.

This time, I had to scrub and polish all the cutlery. It was like a double punishment for me – bringing back, as it did, the memories of the sexual abuse. And as I laid all the spoons, knives and forks back in the drawer, I vowed never to speak to Doris again.

But for some reason, Doris never breathed a word about Nurse Grantham and our midnight feasts. I sometimes wondered if the elderly nurse had put her under a spell. But though she let us clown around a little, Nurse Grantham didn't stand for any real trouble. There was one girl on the ward who liked to wait until we were all dozing off, and then she would throw her slippers or her hairbrush at our heads to wake us up. Occasionally, it would lead to a brawl and then a mass punishment for us all. But Nurse Grantham didn't allow it. She let us have fun, but she also made sure we behaved. There was no bullying or fighting. I loved her, and hoped she knew how much we appreciated her good heart. In some ways, she reminded me of my Scottish granny, and on those occasions, I was enveloped by a rush of sadness and homesickness. But those small kindnesses, set against a backdrop of evil and despair, meant the world to me.

*****

At Aston Hall, our birthdays were marked with a cake, baked in the kitchens, and the girls would gather round and sing the rudest version of *Happy Birthday* they could possibly get away with.

Afterwards, it was bumps on the hard wooden floor in the hall, which was more of a curse than a present. We were not allowed any contact with the outside world so there were no cards from family or friends. That said, my own family had never bothered much with my birthday anyway, so I didn't feel as though I was missing out. Some of the girls were barely even aware when their birthdays came around until they were presented with a cake.

Inevitably, days and dates all merged and mulched into one. We had no way of marking time, no structure or variety to our days, and so each was much like the next. And, of course, we were pumped full of Largactil every day. Time often seemed to slow down to a complete stop, with all the medication we had to swallow. The world looked so hazy and dull. It was as if everything was happening in slow-motion. So, it was no wonder that celebrations almost passed us by. But my birthday came four days before Christmas, and so it was impossible for me ever to forget it.

In December 1970, I was due to turn 17. That week, a real Christmas tree arrived in the big hall, and Sister

Clackton brought boxes overflowing with tinsel and baubles from the storeroom.

"Any fighting, and you're back in bed," she warned.

We loved decorating the tree, if only as a distraction. We made paper chains too, sticking together endless strips of gummy coloured paper, and stringing them from one wall to another. By the time we had finished, the room looked splendidly festive. Part of me was brimming with excitement. It was Christmas, after all. But I also felt a deep sadness. This room looked like a hub of celebration and happiness. But the fairy lights and the baubles were all for show, we knew that. There was no festive cheer in the treatment room.

The Salvation Army came in and sang carols in the hallway, whilst we listened, transfixed. I had always loved church music. I remembered my uncle's bagpipes in Scotland, and I remembered the gospel choir, near my home, and I was transported to a happier, safer place.

"We wish you a Merry Christmas," sang the choir, with no idea at all of the misery and anguish that awaited us.

Looking back, I wonder why none of us shouted out, why we didn't scream at the top of our voices about the abuse. Surely someone in the choir would have listened and taken notice? Dr Milner, though, was a top psychiatrist and even the nurses fawned over him as if he was Santa himself. So how would anyone hold him to account, less still someone in a community choir? The truth was, I think we were all past caring about ourselves. We didn't shout out because there was no point. The message was clear, we simply didn't matter.

On my birthday, Sandy led the other girls in singing *Happy Birthday* and bumping me 17 times on the parquet floor.

"Enough!" I yelled. "My bum isn't fat enough for all these bumps!"

It was a bittersweet day. I could hardly believe that I was 17 years old. Whilst other girls my age were learning to drive, going to college and having babies in the real world, we were stuck in a zombie-like hell. We were almost frozen in time. We might as well have been preserved in formaldehyde.

But the day after my birthday, we held a Christmas party, and we were allowed to play music in the hallway. And on Christmas Eve some of the girls and the younger nurses put on a festive play.

I could almost – almost – have kidded myself that this was a happy time, and that the Christmas spirit was here in Aston Hall after all. Later on Christmas Eve, Nurse Grantham arrived for the night shift, bringing chocolates and sweets for us all.

"These must have cost you a fortune, buying for all us lot," I marvelled. "Thank you."

Christmas morning dawned and despite everything, there was excitement in the air. Local charities had donated gifts for us all: apples, oranges, small chocolate Santas. There were dollies for the younger ones.

"I've more presents this year than I usually get at home," I said to Sandy.

"Me as well," she replied, unwrapping a set of bath smellies.

We exchanged Christmas cards with each other, but there were none from the outside world. After breakfast, as usual, we were given a dose of sedative, to keep us quiet.

"I wonder how many other kids are drugged up on Christmas morning?" Sandy yawned.

There wasn't a single day off from the medication; weekends, birthdays, Christmas. We were drugged up and shut up, and it seemed like nobody cared. But despite everything, we made the most of our Christmas Day. We were so used to the sedation by now, that we had more or less forgotten how it felt to be without it. And Christmas dinner was sumptuous. Yorkshire puddings, beef and roast potatoes. Afterwards we still had to wash up and sweep the floors, there was no escaping our chores. Yet I didn't mind that in the least. The rest of the country was no doubt washing a pile of dirty pots, just as we were. Just like us, they were probably full of roast potatoes and feeling sick after a second helping of Christmas pudding. It felt good to be connected in some small way to the outside world.

*****

"Mackie!" shouted a voice, shrill and insistent.

My stomach somersaulted. It was a grey afternoon, early in 1971, and I was being summoned into the office to see Sister Clackton. It was around 2pm, not the usual time for Milner. Besides, he had already chosen his prey for the day. But maybe I was extra, squeezed into the day's schedule? Whatever it was she wanted, I knew it would not be good. Nervously, I pulled at my fingers and flicked my head from side to side. But when she opened her mouth, I was pleasantly surprised.

"You've got a little job in the sewing room," she told me. "We need a responsible girl to help out there."

She must have seen the excitement in my eyes and was quick to quash it.

"Responsible, mind," she rapped. "Any messing and you're back here, sharpish."

I nodded meekly and didn't smile, despite myself.

"You lucky cow, Carol," said the other girls. "Sewing has got to be better than sitting here all day."

Some of the younger girls did go off to be taught lessons sometimes, but I had never been chosen. This was my first chance to leave Laburnum Ward and I was determined not to mess it up.

The next morning, after breakfast, one of the nurses escorted me outside, down the driveway, to a little building on the right. It was a joy just to be outside, feeling the drizzle and the chill wind through my thin blouse.

"Here's the sewing room," she told me. "Be a good girl now, Mackie."

The sewing teacher, Mrs Turner, was a diminutive woman with dark hair, smartly dressed and very posh indeed. She showed me to my sewing machine, a Singer treadle, and ran through the basic instructions. There were around 10 other girls in the room, all busy sewing. There were some from my ward and some who I didn't know at all. Some had physical disabilities, others, like me, were probably deemed not capable of more complex tasks. But I didn't mind one bit. It was an outing, coming to the sewing room. That first morning flew by and I soon got the hang of threading up my machine and feeding the blue material steadily under the needle.

"We're making pyjamas for the patients today," Mrs Turner told me. "When you've mastered those, Miss Mackie, we shall move on to sewing uniforms for the nurses."

I was mesmerised by the way she spoke. I'd never heard anyone so well-to-do in all my life.

"I shall certainly try my very, very best," I answered, with the biggest plum in my mouth that I could find.

The teacher ignored me, but I collapsed into a fit of giggles afterwards and unfortunately ran a seam right across the front of a pyjama jacket. Mrs Turner tutted and rolled her eyes, but she was not the type of woman to lose her temper, I could see that. Her only real weakness was her two sausage dogs which, strangely, were allowed to accompany her to work each day. I hated them. They nipped my feet as I worked the treadle and it hurt. One day, one of them took a bite at my toe and I kicked out in frustration.

"Don't you go upsetting my little doggies," admonished Mrs Turner. "Or I shall report back to Sister Clackton."

I knew Clacko was not as soft as Mrs Turner, so I decided to put up with the sausage dogs in silence from now on. But I sewed the arms and legs together on the next garment I was making, in silent revenge. In truth, I was actually quite good at sewing, I'd been a homemaker since I was a little girl and I enjoyed crafts. The days passed quickly whilst I was working there, too. I would maybe sew Monday to Friday for three or four weeks in a row, and then have a break of two weeks, because there was no more work to do. But I always looked forward to going back there. As time went on, I was trusted to walk to the sewing room alone, without a nurse.

"No funny business, mind," Sister Clackton reminded me.

Sometimes, as I walked down the path towards the sewing room, a stray thought would flash into my mind: should I make a dash for it – should I run away? It was such a temptation. But then, I would remember the fate of the poor drowned boy who besieged my dreams at night. I remembered Tania, who was carted off to a borstal or worse after running away. And, though I didn't want to admit it, even to myself, where would I go? I couldn't go home. Ian was there. And besides, my mother didn't want me. Almost imperceptibly, I was becoming institutionalised. I was becoming frightened of facing the outside world. "Better the devil you know," I said to myself. But in my case, there were two devils; here and at home. Despite myself, that thought made me laugh. I was spoilt for choice. I pushed all thoughts of escaping away and concentrated on my sewing instead. And by the time I finished working there, I could sew, knit and crochet, skills I would carry with me throughout the rest of my life.

I had probably been sewing for around three months when Sister Clackton again called me to the office in the middle of the day.

"You are one of our long-standing patients now, Mackie," she told me. "Did you realise that?"

I nodded. Girls came and went from the ward, sometimes they were shipped off to higher security units, occasionally, perhaps, they went back home. We never really knew what happened to them. Possibly it was something far more sinister. But gradually the old, familiar faces were disappearing and newer, younger girls were arriving.

"By and large, your behaviour has been very good," Clackton added.

I thought back to me squeezing the cat out of the window. I remembered smashing the window blocks to let Tania and Suzy escape. But I said nothing. And it was hard not to smile when I thought of all the rice pudding skin I had thrown under the table for the dog.

"So, we've decided it will be your job to go the village shop," she continued. "You will be given a list of newspapers and light shopping required by the nursing staff. You will go straight to the shop, you will speak to nobody and on no account – on absolutely no account – must you deviate from the route. Understood?"

I nodded. My mind was swirling. I was being allowed out into the world, on my own. This was different than simply going to the sewing room, which was part of the Aston Hall complex. I was going to see other people – normal people. I wasn't sure I could take on the challenge. I wasn't even sure I wanted to go. It seemed overwhelming. My face must have betrayed my anxieties because Clackton rapped:

"This is a position of great trust. You are *extremely* lucky."

Yes, wasn't I just. I could never forget that. The next day, after breakfast, I was handed a list and a purse. I was under orders to walk to the shop, in Aston-on-Trent village, and return with the goods.

"No messing around or I will find out!" said Sister Clackton quietly into my ear.

As the large front door clanged behind me, I felt lightheaded, as though my feet weren't touching the ground. And the walk up the drive, towards the main road, seemed endless. I was absolutely exhausted by the time I reached the road.

For two years, I had been cooped up inside, with no exercise, no daylight and pumped full of drugs. It was hardly a surprise that I was weak and my muscles had wasted away.

In the village, it was so completely normal it appeared bizarre and contrived to me. There were people out shopping and a couple of cars went past down the high street. One elderly lady was out in her garden, fussing over some flowers. I felt my skin prickle – it seemed as though everyone was watching me. I knew that they could tell I was from Aston Hall, just from my shabby, ill-fitting clothes and my pale face. I was like a plant which had been kept indoors for far too long. I was sure my behaviour was a giveaway too, my intermittent twitches and tics and the anxious way I stared around me. I tried hard to blend in, but I just couldn't. I felt so out of place. Most of the villagers walked by without a word. But an old lady smiled and said:

"Good morning, my dear. How are you?"

The pleasantry stumped me. The question itself was so unexpected that I had no idea how to reply. I couldn't remember the last time anyone had asked me how I was. Certainly not at Aston Hall – not at home, either. I mumbled something in reply and smiled nervously back at her.

"Lovely day," she said. "Are you off for a walk?"

I was so taken aback that I scurried off quickly without a word and into the village shop. The shopkeeper was friendly too, taking my list from me and filling my shopping bag with various newspapers, magazines and snacks. I managed to get everything I needed, and I got back to Aston Hall without a single hiccup. Nurse Clackton of course did not offer any praise, but neither was I punished, so to me the trip had been an unmitigated success.

At the end of the week I made another trip, again for the same supplies. I saw the elderly lady and she gave me a cheery wave. The shopkeeper nodded his recognition too.

"Back again," he commented.

I just nodded dumbly. I wasn't used to making conversation and small talk. I wasn't used to adults speaking to me at all, unless it was an order or an insult. It was all rather new and rather odd. But by my third or fourth jaunt, I was beginning to quite enjoy myself. I was gaining in confidence and strength. I could feel that the long walks were paying off physically, but it was mentally that I felt so much brighter. The other girls on the ward were so envious.

"Why not bring us back a few sweets, Carol," they cajoled. "Go on, nobody would miss a few pence. Just tag a bar of chocolate onto your order. Or a packet of Benson and Hedges. Go on!"

But I dared not. In all the months that I did the shopping trips – sometimes up to three times a week – I did not pinch as much as a jellybean. I was too afraid. I never diverted at all from the route either, not even to pick a buttercup or a dandelion. I felt, somehow, that I was being watched, and that if I had put one single step out of line, I would have been caught. It was as though Sister Clackton had a giant eye in the sky, tracking my every move. Sometimes, I could almost feel her breath on my neck. When I stopped to wave at the old lady in her garden, I could almost hear Clackton, hissing down my ear:

"That's enough, Mackie. Keep walking…"

One day, as I packed newspapers into my bag, the shopkeeper gave me a sympathetic smile and said to me:

"We know it's not a very nice place, Aston Hall."

I was a little disappointed that he knew, without question, that I was a patient there. I had hoped that recently I was carrying this shopping lark off quite well. But now that he had brought it up, this was my chance, my chance to tell somebody. I had waited years for this. I had fantasised about someone coming to rescue me. But now that the moment was here, it was rather underwhelming and I simply stared mutely. Then, without another word, I turned and walked back out into the fresh air.

All the way back, my heart thudded and my pulse raced. Part of me was worried that it was a trap set by Sister Clackton and that the shopkeeper was one of her stooges. But in reality, I didn't speak out for the same reason that I didn't run away. My spirit had been crushed, my voice had been silenced. I was little more than a carcass, for Milner to pick off what he wanted and discard the bones. I could not confide in the shopkeeper because I was no longer sure what exactly it was I wanted to say.

Chapter Fourteen

I had been complaining of toothache for some time, and every morning, when I cleaned my teeth, my gums bled. At first, I kept my pain to myself. All ailments were treated within the walls of Aston Hall; we never left the place unless it was strictly necessary. The joke amongst the girls was that all early exits were in wooden boxes only. Besides, I didn't want Milner poking around inside my mouth. I would rather simply put up with the pain. From time to time, I suffered with sore throats, and sometimes it was so painful I could hardly swallow. But I never told Sister Clackton. I was frightened of what might happen, and I reckoned a sore throat was preferable to more torture from Dr Milner.

But this toothache was different, and as the weeks passed, it grew worse and worse. I could barely eat. And one morning, when we got up, Sandy said:

"Look at the state of your lips, Carol! They're so swollen!"

I was too poorly to eat breakfast and later I was taken

to see a dentist, in a small room just outside the ward. He looked inside my mouth, sighed and shook his head.

"She's clearly had a very poor diet for years," he said. "And her oral hygiene is poor also. I'm not sure we can save these teeth."

I hadn't even owned a toothbrush as a kid. My mind flashed back to those desperate scenes in our cramped family bathroom, me swilling my mouth with antiseptic after the abuse by Ian.

"They'll have to come out," the dentist decided. "The whole lot."

I was diagnosed with pyrea, a severe form of gum disease. I was given painkillers until my next appointment, but they didn't help, and I was in agony. I was told I'd be having all of my teeth out at once, which seemed drastic, but I wasn't in a position to argue.

The surgery took place under general anaesthetic, again in a small room in another part of Aston Hall. I didn't really mind losing my teeth. But the thought of being knocked out gave me the shivers. I knew what regularly happened when I was unconscious. But this time there was no sign of Dr Milner. And the dentist seemed interested only in my mouth. When I awoke later, my mouth was swollen and sore. But down below, to my relief, I felt absolutely fine. I had all my clothes on, and everything seemed normal.

But days later, when the pain subsided, I still couldn't

eat or speak properly, because I had no teeth at all. It took several weeks for me to be fitted with dentures, and then even longer for me to get used to them.

"I feel like I have a set of piano keys inside my mouth," I told Sandy. "They're so uncomfortable."

I wasn't the only girl who lost her teeth in Aston Hall. Many of us had such poor health that our teeth simply rotted. And yet at 17, I was much too young for dentures. It felt like another loss, another blow, another piece of me stolen away by Dr Milner.

One morning, as we tidied up after breakfast, Sister Clackton came into the dining room and shouted: "Form an orderly line upstairs. You will each be seen, one by one, in the treatment room."

A deathly hush descended on the room. It was like someone had thrown a fire blanket over us.

"It can't be the truth drug," I whispered to Sandy. "Not if we're all going."

Even so, our skin crawled with a collective dread as we waited and fidgeted in the queue.

"Quiet!" ordered Sister Clackton. "Quiet or you will be severely punished!"

She slammed the dining room door hard behind her and we heard her shouting in the corridor outside.

"What's got into Clacko?" whispered the girl behind me. "Looks like Milner's working overtime."

When it was my turn to go inside, I noticed there was a

standard hospital bed, in place of the usual grimy mattress on the floor.

"Remove your undergarments and climb onto the bed, Mackie," said Dr Milner. "It's just a swab, it won't take a moment."

I had no idea what a swab was. I tensed all my muscles and braced myself for an assault, screwing up my eyes and clenching my jaw. I couldn't understand why I hadn't been anaesthetised, as normal. I felt a quick, sharp pain down below, and then he simply said:

"All done. Come on. Don't dally, Mackie."

I didn't need telling twice. I scrambled off the bed and grabbed my knickers, hastily pulling them up under my skirt. I felt like I'd got away with something.

Afterwards, back on the ward, the other girls were filled with indignation and disgust.

"It was a gonorrhoea test," said one.

"Where would we get gonorrhoea from?" asked another.

"From Milner! The dirty old git!" replied the first girl. "I bet he's been passing it round all of us. That's why he wants us to get checked out. He's the problem, not us."

I had no idea what gonorrhoea was. I'd never even heard of it.

"Does it kill you?" I asked in a small voice.

The other girls rolled their eyes and giggled.

"Nah," they laughed. "It's just a sexually transmitted disease. You'll be fine."

171

But I spent many nights, lying awake, worrying about the test, and hoping I was going to be OK. I didn't like the sound of it. Eventually, I plucked up courage to ask Sister Clackton for my results.

"None of your business, Mackie," she snapped.

I shrank back, confused. If it wasn't my business, then whose was it?

*****

Later that same year, and not long before my 18th birthday, Sister Clackton collared me one morning and made an announcement which sent a chill right through me.

"You're going home for a visit this weekend, Mackie," she said. "Pack a bag. You will be given one change of clothes. Be in my office for 3pm today."

I stared dumbly at her. I felt so torn that there was actually a physical pain in my chest, as though I was being pulled, one way and another. I was desperate to see my younger siblings. I couldn't wait to take in their faces, to see how they had grown, to ask if they'd missed me. But I couldn't even think about seeing Ian. The monster who had ruined my childhood twice over. It was as a result of his abuse that I had found myself in Aston Hall – and victim to more abuse. How would I react to him now?

"Home?" I said uncertainly. "What, me?"

"It's standard procedure to have home visits before

discharge," Sister Clackton said, busy tidying papers on her desk. "3pm sharp. Today. Come on now Mackie, out of my way."

I wasn't sure whether I could refuse the visit. I didn't want to go. Even the idea of being in the same house as Ian was terrifying. I hadn't thought about him for months, not consciously anyway, although I still wet the bed most nights and I still shuddered when I had to count the cutlery. But by and large, I pretended he didn't exist and that the abuse had never happened. The trauma had been mothballed and pushed to a dusty corner of my mind. Until now.

Of course, at nearly 20 years of age, there was every possibility he might have left home, but somehow I doubted it. I couldn't imagine Ian settling down with a good job and his own place. No, he would still be there alright. The resident bully. At 3pm, I returned to the office as instructed, my stomach by now roiling in protest, my head twitching and nodding uncontrollably. I pulled at my fingers so hard I thought the joints might snap.

Then, through the heavy silence, the doorbell.

I jumped like I had been scalded. Outside, I caught a glimpse of Dad's van, with F.B. Atkins written on the side. Sister Clackton went to answer and sent him back outside to wait in the van.

"Gather your things," she told me ceremoniously, flapping her arms, as though I had an entire set of luxury suitcases. In reality, I had a tatty old bag containing a change of socks and underwear.

"Back for Sunday, 5pm sharp," she said. "And not a minute later."

I nodded and walked outside. Strangely, I was nervous to see my father. I didn't want my emotions to spill over, I couldn't afford that. It had been over a year since his fleeting visit to Aston Hall, and on that occasion we hadn't even spoken.

"Carol!" he yelled when he spotted me.

Part of me wanted so much to run over and throw my arms around him. But I could not. It was as if I was bound by an invisible force field and I could not bear to have physical contact with any other human being, not even my own dad. Even the thought of sitting next to him in the van filled with me with dread. I shrank back and nodded, politely, before opening the passenger side door. But then, all at once, I was bowled over by an over-excited bundle of fur, yapping and barking and licking my face.

"Peter!" I laughed. "You remember me, don't you boy."

"He remembers you all right," Dad smiled. "He spent months sitting at the window after you went."

I was glad of the diversion, and maybe Dad was, too. Peter was so giddy and noisy that he dominated the entire journey home.

"He's missed you, the little dog," Dad said. "We all have."

I stiffened at the thought. I knew exactly why Ian might have missed me and again, I was frozen with fear.

"Is Ian still there?" I ventured.

It was the first time I had said his name out loud for years and it was hard.

"Oh yeah," Dad replied enthusiastically. "I got him a job at my place, driving, but he got the sack. He's at home. Everyone is. They're all waiting for you."

A shiver ran through me and I leaned my head against the cool glass of the passenger window. It was surreal, driving along roads which had once been so familiar to me, but now seemed like an alien landscape. It had been two and half years since I'd even been inside a car. So many times, I had longed to escape Aston Hall, but now that I was out, I felt perversely afraid and apprehensive. I was vulnerable, somehow, without those terrible walls around me.

"I drove all over Derby looking for you after you left," Dad carried on. "I'd been to so many places by the time I got to Aston Hall that time. Did you see me outside, in the van? They threatened to call the police if I didn't leave. I didn't know where they had taken you, or why. It's been so awful. I've missed you, nuisance, I really have. Must be a relief, though, to be coming home for the weekend. You must be thrilled."

I smiled at the use of my old nickname and nodded in agreement.

"Yes, thrilled," I repeated in a flat voice.

I could not have told him the truth. It would have broken his heart.

*****

We rounded the corner into Millom Place, and as I spotted our old red front door at the end of the cul-de-sac, with steps leading down, the paving flags cracked and poking with weeds, my mouth ran dry. This was it. Dad bounded out of the van, closely followed by Peter, and I trailed behind. I felt sick inside. I knew I should be angry. Ready to face Ian and vent my fury. It was his fault, after all, that I had been incarcerated for all this time. Without his abuse, I would never have run away, I would never have been taken into care.

As Dad opened the front door I was hit by the familiar and unsettling smell of home, a mix of greasy chips and stale cigarettes. The hall floor, just plain bitumen, needed sweeping. We couldn't afford a carpet. Yet we could buy a caravan. The juxtaposition made me indignant, even now, after so long away. We didn't have a vacuum cleaner either, and I could see from the dust balls and clumps of mud and dried-up food that Mum hadn't thought to sweep up lately.

"Go the Mackie's and get mucky."

The song was as apt as ever. After the cleanliness of Aston Hall, the filth of my family home was even more striking. It was like a refuse heap. In the living room, Mum sat on the sofa, with her leg bandaged, staring at what could only be the wall opposite.

"Hello," I said stiffly.

"Alright," she said, not even standing up to greet me.

I hovered in the doorway, believing there might be more to come. I hoped she might say something. Anything. But it seemed not.

My stomach was churning and I could feel sweat dripping down my back. The stress of finding myself back in my own home, faced with my mother, was almost too much to take. But for Mum, this seemed to be an unremarkable situation. I almost felt as though I was taking up her time. I would have preferred anger and hostility, rather than complete indifference. I felt as though she didn't care much about my presence, one way or the other. I had been away for so long and we had so much catching up to do. But despite that, or perhaps because of that, we said nothing at all.

I wandered into the kitchen where Ava and the twins were all waiting. Ava threw out her arms and hugged me in a tidal wave of emotion.

"Oh, we've missed you," she squealed. "Where the hell have you been?"

"Aston Hall," I replied, uncomfortable with the embrace. I just wasn't used to it.

"Is it because you ran away?" asked one of the twins.

I shrugged, awkwardly.

"How long are you home for?" asked Clare, her face bobbing at the doorway.

"Just the weekend I think," I said.

It was only two days and yet the time stretched ahead of me, impossibly. I felt on edge – waiting, watching constantly for him to appear. This was my home and yet I did not feel I belonged here at all. The chip pan was on the stove, there was washing draped half-heartedly on a rack by the fire. It was all exactly the same as when I had left. And yet for me, everything had changed.

For a while, I chatted with the younger ones in the kitchen and marvelled at how tall they'd grown, how mature they seemed. I had missed out on so much. Then, from the living room, came Mum's voice.

"Right, I'm off to bingo."

I had expected no better, but it stung nonetheless. I was home. I was back. And yet she could not miss a night's bingo. That evening, I slotted back into my old role of cooking and cleaning. But when I opened the cutlery drawer – and saw the offending utensils glaring at me – I froze. I was momentarily stuck in time, as flashbacks of Ian pinning me down ran through my mind.

"Everything OK?" Ava asked.

I nodded brightly.

"Yes course," I replied.

Later, when it was time for bed, I stood at the bottom of our staircase and stared at the beige swirly wallpaper and the worn carpet, so dirty and threadbare the colour was no longer discernible. And I saw, just for a moment, the ghost of a little girl, nothing more than a shadowy sprite, skipping up the steps with a bundle of laundry in her arms, blissfully unaware of the brutal horror that awaited her at the top.

"If you grass, you'll get it twice as bad. So lie still…"

That night in bed was like waiting for a surgical operation. The suspense was awful. I was back in my own bedroom, with my sisters, painfully aware that my nemesis was sleeping just a few feet away, through the next wall. I still hadn't come face to face with him. He was there alright, but hadn't left his bedroom the whole evening. But I knew I couldn't avoid him forever.

"Tell us about Aston Hall," whispered Ava through the darkness. "Is it fun? What do you do all day?"

I would have loved to have shared my burden, especially with my sister, with someone who cared for me. But once again, just as with the shopkeeper in the village, I clammed up. It was as though someone had wired my false teeth together.

"I'm tired, duck," I mumbled, forcing a yawn. "Let's get some sleep."

The next morning, as usual, I had wet the bed.

"Ugh, Carol, you dirty cow," Margaret sneered. "You're too old for this. I've told you before."

"I have problems," I snapped. "You have no idea. None at all."

I needed a bath to wash off the stale urine, but I was too afraid to be in the bathroom, naked and alone. I felt vulnerable. Exposed.

"Will you sit on the loo whilst I have a bath and keep me company?" I asked Ava.

If she thought it was strange, she didn't say so. Ava had a kind heart. And she and I were close, so I think she was happy to follow me around. Or perhaps she knew full well what Ian had done to me? Perhaps everyone knew, but like me, she dare not say it out loud. Ours was a secret which screamed, silently, from every room in our house, from every window, every wall. Our family was riddled with it.

"Ooh, Carol, I think you've put on a bit of weight whilst you've been away," Ava said, as I ran the hot water. "You look better. Not so skinny."

Obligingly, she sat on the loo seat and chatted away, while I got washed and then dressed. All that day, I made her come with me, every time I had to go upstairs. She was like my own personal bodyguard. Sometimes, I fancied I could see Ian's shadow on the landing, waiting to pounce. I could sense his eyes boring into me, with that faintly mocking look that he had when he was torturing me.

"You're so jumpy," Ava noticed. "What's got into you, Carol?"

I shook my head.

"Don't know," I lied. "Just strange being home, I suppose."

She was right, I was a nervous wreck. The social worker had taken me to Aston Hall because she claimed I was disturbed. Well, now I was well and truly deranged. The irony was bitter.

Mum cleared off to bingo again on Saturday. I wanted it not to matter. But it hurt. Oh, how it hurt. Even though I was used to such rejection. I pushed it to the edges of my mind and instead saw my pals, spent time with the younger kids, and then helped cook the evening meal.

"Just like old times," Dad smiled, as I served a cottage pie.

On Sunday afternoon, just a couple of hours before I was due to leave, it happened.

Ian came into the kitchen.

My heart was hammering so loudly against my ribs, I felt sure he could hear it. He looked at me, briefly, but didn't speak. I held my breath, and time stood still, as he got himself a drink and then disappeared. It lasted only a couple of minutes, but it felt like another episode of abuse, even though he hadn't touched me. He hadn't even spoken to me.

I bit back tears, furious with myself that I had allowed him to reduce me to rubble like this. I had built the meeting up in my mind to such an extent that even when nothing happened, I was distraught. He was ruining my life every day, even now.

There was no food left in the cupboards, so I had bread

and crisps before Dad checked his watch and announced it was time to drive me back to Aston Hall. One by one, I hugged all my sisters goodbye.

"Can't believe I'm leaving again," I said sadly.

In truth, I could not wait to get back there. It wounded me that I was not wanted at home. Dad had no excuse now, he knew where I was. He must know why I was there. So why did he not try to bring me home? Why was he taking me back without so much as an objection? When we pulled up outside Laburnum Ward, I hopped quickly out of the van before he could try to embrace me. I couldn't bear close proximity from a man, but neither could I bear to explain why.

"Bye!" I called casually, as though he was just dropping me off at the local shops.

I rang the doorbell and waited for Sister Clackton, and my thoughts jumbled in my mind. I did not want to stay at home with my family. But I wanted my family to want me to stay. Both places were torture. Both places were evil. Perhaps because home was the place where I was supposed to feel safe, I felt the violation more keenly there. The people who were supposed to love and protect me had let me down, and that was so hard. At Aston Hall, although the level of abuse was worse, the perpetrators were not people I had once loved and trusted.

As it was, I was caught between the devil and the devil. With nothing in between.

Chapter Fifteen

Two Fridays later, I was called again into the office and informed I would be going home for another weekend visit.

Part of me dreaded seeing Ian, as before. But this time, I was also looking forward to seeing my younger siblings again. I had thought a lot about home since my first visit and I felt stronger. I realised there was so much I missed that I hadn't been aware of, the tatty old front door, the neighbours waving as I passed, the stale smell of the chip-pan on the stove. They were familiar to me, they reminded me of another life and I had missed them. Yes, the house was dirty and smelly, but it was my house. The family was fractured and dysfunctional, but it was my family all the same. Now that I had faced Ian once, I felt I could do it again.

"Can't wait," I told Sister Clackton. "Is my dad coming to collect me?"

She nodded. I was given my morning medicine as usual, but then Dad arrived slightly early and I missed my second and third dose. I skipped out through the front door smiling at the thought of pulling the wool over Clacko's eyes for once.

When I got home, there was no acknowledgement from Mum again, just as I expected. My siblings were pleased to see me, but there was no celebration, no huge welcome. Certainly no empathy with my plight. By the following morning, I could feel a frustration and an anger boiling inside me. Normally, I was tanked up on sedatives. But now, I was jittery and full of energy. I felt as though I was seeing the world with a new clarity. That afternoon, before she left for bingo, Mum said to me, "I want you gone by the time I get back."

"It's only Saturday!" I protested. "I don't go back until tomorrow."

She glared at me and I felt myself snap. The injustice was too much to bear.

"Why do I have to go back there anyway?" I yelled. "Why?"

Mum didn't even look at me.

"You have behavioural problems, that's why," she replied, in a flat, toneless voice.

Furiously, I began kicking out at the chairs and furniture. I ran at my siblings, lashing out, hitting anyone who came within an arm's length of me. It was like I was possessed. If she thought I had problems, then I wouldn't disappoint.

"Why do you think I have behavioural problems?" I

screamed. "You know what happened to me. You know. I told the truth and you said I'd lied."

My siblings watched, wide-eyed and horrified from the door, waiting for the revelation. But it never came. The words withered and died in my throat. Once again, I could not share my deepest torment.

"You know," I said again, but by now, I was whimpering and sobbing, falling to my knees with my head in my hands.

"Leave her alone," Dad said, ushering everyone into the kitchen. "Leave her be."

From the hallway, I heard Mum's voice, as she buttoned up her coat.

"I want her gone tonight. I'm going to be late for bingo now."

But Dad stood his ground. I did not return to Aston Hall until Sunday, as arranged. But all that night and the following day, my siblings bunched together and whispered about me.

"Watch her, she's a nutter."

"Carol's gone mad, she's dangerous."

"She needs to go back to the hospital."

Late on Saturday night, when I was in bed, I heard the front door slam and I knew Ian was home. I lay in bed, as stiff and tense as an ironing board, as he climbed noisily up the stairs and into his bedroom.

All night I lay awake, suffocated by the place. I was filled with energy and with rage. After the airy spaces and large wards at Aston Hall, the house seemed poky and stuffy. I longed to be out of there. But I refused to be bullied out of there either.

I would stand my ground.

Out in the yard the next morning, a neighbour poked her head over the fence and I heard her say, "That girl next door has problems, you know. She's a real lunatic."

Wearily, I began to think that perhaps they were all right. Maybe I did belong in the asylum, after all.

*****

Over the years, I had watched as the older girls, one by one, were released out into the world. Nobody stayed at Aston Hall past the age of 18, except for Doris of course. And so, in December 1971, when I finally turned 18, I knew that my time there was almost over. I couldn't wait to get out of that place. And yet, I was strangely apprehensive, too.

Eighteen was a landmark birthday. A time to take stock of achievements and of relationships. Yet for me, it was all about lack and loss. The date seemed only to emphasise what I didn't have, what I had lost, what I had not achieved. I was 18, but I had spent much of my life as a lab rat, being poked and prodded and injected and abused by whoever fancied a go.

Early in the new year of 1972, Clackton called me into

the office and I knew, before she spoke, what was coming.

"It's time for you to leave us, Carol," she said. "I'd like you to pack your things quickly. The social worker will be arriving shortly to take you to Craigmore Hostel."

I stared at her in confusion. I had presumed I would be going home.

"Why can't I go home?" I asked. "I don't want to go to a hostel. I want to go home."

Sister Clackton either didn't hear my question or she didn't feel it worthy of a response.

"Don't forget to strip your bed and wipe it down, ready for the new arrival," Clackton barked as I left the office.

I was in a daze. I couldn't believe what was happening to me. I had no idea why I wasn't allowed to go home, whether my mother had refused to have me back, or whether Dr Milner had vetoed it. I had behaved well at Aston Hall, I had good reports from the sewing room and my trips to the village had all passed without a problem. Surely I could be trusted on my own?

Back on the ward, the other girls gathered around, wishing me well and giving me goodbye hugs. Sandy sat on her bed, sobbing. I had never seen her so upset.

"Don't go, Carol," she pleaded. "Please, don't go."

I shrugged helplessly.

"It's not up to me, is it," I said, biting back my own tears. "I'm not even going home, Sandy, I'm going to some hostel or other."

"Not Craigmore?" asked one of the girls.

I nodded.

"That's Milner's place," she said.

The words sent a chill through me. The blood seemed to solidify in my veins. I was going from the frying pan, to the fire. It was like a repeat of last time, leaving behind the abuse at home to be abused at Aston Hall instead. But this time, I was leaving behind all of my friends. It was yet another cruel blow.

It didn't take me long to pack my belongings. A few toiletries and a hairbrush. Sandy and I clung to each other when Miss Clark, the social worker, came to collect me. I hadn't seen her once since she had brought me to Aston Hall, almost three years earlier, and her face was set solid, like concrete, just the same as I remembered.

"I'll miss you," I told Sandy.

"Me too," she said.

And then it was time. Off into the unknown once again. Leaving all of my friends behind was worse in some ways than leaving my family. They had become my family. We were more like sisters – bound together by horror and trauma, but bound together just the same.

As we pulled away, down the drive and Aston Hall became just a dot in the driver's mirror, I felt an overwhelming sadness. Strangely, I could only remember the happy times. The late night chats, the pillow fights, the secret cigarettes with Nurse Grantham. I would miss the

gang, and Sandy more than anyone. And I had no idea why
I was being carted off to yet another institution.

"Why can't I go home?" I demanded. "Why do I have
to go to Dr Milner's hostel? I'm 18 years old. I'm an adult.
Why can't I do what I like?"

"You are a sexual deviant," said Miss Clark,
disapprovingly. "That's why you ended up in Aston Hall in
the first place. You're not fit to look after yourself."

I didn't even know what a sexual deviant was. But I felt
that she had a ready answer for every objection I made. My
future was already decided and I had no say in it.

We soon arrived at the hostel, a large, miserable
building, like an old-fashioned workhouse, with a wall
around it. As we got out of the car, Miss Clark handed me
a plastic carrier bag.

"There's a new dress and cardigan in there and a
change of underwear," she said.

"Thanks," I replied, taken aback at her uncharacteristic
kindness.

"Oh, don't thank me," she said, her eyes narrowing.
"It's standard practice. Bought with state money, too."

She knocked on the door. I stood behind her. When her
sharp knock was answered, my mouth fell open in surprise.
I came face to face with Miss Halliwell, the superintendent
from The Cedars Remand Home.

"You chopped my finger off!" I blurted out. "What are
you doing here?"

I was speaking out of turn, but my astonishment had got the better of me.

"You can't speak to me like that," rapped Miss Halliwell. "You ought to have respect for people in authority."

She grabbed my shoulder and steered me inside, into an entrance hall with a red tiled floor.

"You'll behave yourself whilst you're under my care," she hissed. "Or else."

Something reared up inside me. No longer was I a frightened child, terrified of authority. I'd had nearly three years to see sense. Three years to lose all faith in the people who were supposed to 'look after me'. I was wise enough to keep quiet, to avoid punishment. But I didn't crumble and dissolve every time I was told off. I kept my head up and stared straight back at her.

"Or else," she repeated, smoothing down her tweed skirt with her hands. I wondered idly if it was the same skirt she'd worn at The Cedars. It certainly looked like it.

I was just starting to think what a dreadful mess I was in, when walking down the stairs, I recognised Julie, one of the girls from Aston Hall.

"Alright Carol," she smiled. "Fancy seeing you here! I heard we had a new girl coming, didn't realise it was you though."

Miss Halliwell was busy chatting to Miss Clark, so she simply waved me away and said:

"Show Carol her room, she's in with Dolly and Claire."

Chapter Fifteen

As I followed Julie up the stairs, I decided this place couldn't be as bad as the military regime at Aston Hall if Julie was being allowed to settle me in and show me around, all on her own. There was just one upstairs floor, and our first names were on the doors outside.

"This is yours," Julie said, kicking open a door to reveal an old-fashioned room with three metal beds inside, a large wardrobe, and a chest of drawers. The curtains, floor length, were a horrible floral pattern, and the carpet was just as bad.

"The two other girls in here are nice," Julie told me. "It's a lot better than Aston Hall. In fact, you'll recognise five or six of the girls in here. This place is the next stop on the conveyor belt."

"What about Milner?" I asked. "It's his place, isn't it?"

Julie knew exactly what I was asking.

"No treatments here," she said. "He visits, to make sure we're all behaving. He likes to have a little poke at us, through the bars of our cages, but he doesn't touch us."

Then she wiggled her finger, prodding an imaginary hamster, and I laughed.

"As long as you stay the right side of Halliwell, you'll be alright," she said, and then she was off.

I arranged my belongings on a corner of the dressing table; soap, toothpaste, toothbrush. I put my change of clothes into an empty drawer. It was pitiful that this was what I amounted to. This was all I had. I didn't even have a photograph of my family, or my dog. For a time, I stared out of the window onto the street below, looking out for my dad, in his F.B. Atkins van. Looking for a sign that someone cared. Nobody came, as I knew they wouldn't. But I had to look, I just had to. Even though the sight of the empty street broke my heart.

It wasn't long before I heard the familiar noise of girls chatting and bickering on the landing outside.

"Come on, Carol," shouted Julie, popping her head around my door. "It's lunchtime now."

There were around 15 of us in total in the dining room, and Julie was right, I recognised maybe half a dozen faces. Everyone seemed friendly enough as they all fell into what seemed to be a routine of daily tasks.

"Just stick with me," Julie said, as she began laying the tables with cutlery and condiments.

But then Miss Halliwell appeared in the doorway and waggled a short, stubby finger in my direction.

"Over here," she ordered.

She took me into her office and gave me what I knew, by now, was a dose of Largactil. I hated the taste.

"Did you think you'd escaped it?" she asked with a mirthless laugh. "We have to keep you girls quiet or there would be a bloody riot in here."

Back at the lunch table, I quickly got to know everyone's name. Afterwards, we washed up and cleaned the floors and put the tables away. And then we pretty much had the afternoon to ourselves. But here, there were games and books and even chairs to sit on. It was positively luxurious compared to the hardships at Aston Hall. Every time I thought of the place, I remembered the pals I had left behind, and I saw Sandy's tear-stained face in my mind's eye. I felt a pang of sadness. And that night, in bed, I wondered when on earth it would all end, or whether I was destined to live in institutions for the rest of my life, drugged, abused and worst of all, forgotten.

The following day, we spotted Dr Milner's car outside, and there was a ripple of unease through the girls.

"No treatments here," Julie had told me.

But I wasn't convinced. After breakfast, Miss Halliwell called my name and I walked out of the dining room, accompanied by whistles and cheers from the other girls. I felt as though I was going to the gallows, like it was a public hanging. Waiting in the office, was Dr Milner. The same grey hair. The same rimmed glasses. The same cold, dead eyes.

"You're here to be assessed, Mackie," he said, in his low, reasonable voice; always that edge of superiority, too. Perhaps he felt that by being polite he could somehow smooth out the horrors he perpetrated.

"At Craigmore, we will prepare you for your introduction back into society. But I want you to know that if you step out of line in any way at all, you will be taken back to Aston Hall. Do you understand my dear?"

I nodded, head bowed. I didn't move a muscle. In truth, I was waiting for him to bind my hands and feet, I was expecting the strait jacket, the truth drug, the sexual assault. By staying still, perhaps I thought he would forget I was there. If I was no trouble, I might be spared.

"That will be all," he said, in slight irritation, as though I had overstayed my welcome. "Off you go now."

I walked out of the office with my feet barely touching the tiles. I couldn't believe it. I had got away with it! If this was how life was in this hostel, then I felt sure I could cope.

The days settled into weeks and at first I lived in fear of Milner returning to administer another treatment. I just couldn't accept, after three years of the threat hanging over me each day, like an axe, that it was over. The wait – the dread – had been almost as bad as the ordeal itself.

"Are you sure, no treatments? No truth drug? No anaesthetics? Are you sure?"

I asked my room mates so often they grew sick of answering.

As the weeks became months, they assumed a comfortable pattern. Each morning, we were woken at 6am, each night it was lights out by 8pm. Our beds still had to be made with hospital corners, just like before. But at weekends, we could have a lie in and a late breakfast, if we fancied. Here, there was no staff, except for Miss Halliwell. So we had a stack of household chores to do, cooking, washing, ironing and cleaning. All our clothes went into the wash together, supervised by a different girl every time, and so, just as at Aston Hall, I rarely got my own belongings back on laundry day. Soon, I forgot which were mine anyway. It was all part of the erosion process, continuing the stripping away of our self-respect and our individuality.

Back then, I didn't look too deeply into it. I had got used to not having my own clothes and I was kept busy, too, far too busy to dwell on self-pity. I was usually assigned mending and repairs, sewing patches on jeans, darning holes in socks. And I learned, as the months passed, that Halliwell maybe wasn't so bad after all. She was strict, but usually fair. In comparison with Sister Clackton, she actually seemed quite nice. Good behaviour was rewarded with trips out and we were allowed to go to the local shop alone. For me, just being allowed out into the garden to peg out the washing was a treat. The idea of having windows without bars, doors without locks, was a dream. And so a walk to the shop left me giddy with excitement. As long as we got permission from Miss Halliwell, as long as we behaved, there were no problems.

"No bending the rules, mind," she warned. "Straight to the shop, straight back. You have one hour and no more."

I never deviated from that. I didn't even like stepping off the pavement, in case she somehow found out and shipped me back to Aston Hall. It was lovely to feel the spring sunshine on my face, the rain on my nose. It meant so much, just to be a part of the world again. I never once considered running away. But it wasn't just the threat of punishment that kept me in line. By now I had given up the fight completely. I was totally and wholly institutionalised. Unable to think for myself or to break any rules. Besides, where would I have gone? Who would I have turned to? I had by now been at Craigmore for five months and there had been no contact from my family, not even a letter or a phone call. And it never occurred to me to go and visit them on one of my allotted trips out. If I had been caught, I would have been in serious trouble. But more than that, I knew I wasn't wanted at home.

In our spare time, we painted or knitted or did jigsaws. There was no TV in the dining room, but we had a radio and the girls listened to The Rolling Stones and Elton John. There were chairs, too. Not just dining chairs, but lovely, comfortable, squashy seats. When I sank down into a chair, I felt happiness flooding through me.

"I feel like a princess," I beamed, tucking my feet under me. "This is fit for royalty."

I missed the camaraderie of Aston Hall, but the girls at Craigmore were mostly friendly. I made a best pal, Monica. Like me, Monica had been at Aston Hall. She had a shock of ginger hair, freckles and mischievous blue eyes. She and I both shared the same sense of humour. We had learned to laugh at our situation, whether through desperation or self-preservation, or perhaps a mixture of both. Either way, we managed to see the funny side of most things.

Some girls had come from approved schools and borstals and were in and out of trouble. They very often got on the wrong side of Miss Halliwell. One night, she was smoking in her office, and one of them cheekily said:

"Give us a fag, you miserable cow."

It turned out one of them had a contraband box of matches, bought in a trip to the shops and kept hidden between the mattress and the springs of her bed. When Miss Halliwell refused to give them a cigarette, they ran upstairs and set fire to the bedroom curtains. All hell was let loose as the smell of smoke filled the corridors and Miss Halliwell yelled for buckets for water. But though I thoroughly enjoyed the spectacle, I didn't allow myself to get involved. I wanted to stay on the right side of authority. The culprits were grounded for an entire week; they weren't allowed to leave the building, even to go into the garden. The punishment didn't seem too drastic at all to many of us girls. After all, we'd been locked up for years on end at Aston Hall without so much as a sniff of daylight.

Six months into my stay at Craigmore, Miss Halliwell called me into her office.

"You've been doing well so far, Mackie," she told me. "So we've decided to allow you to go to work."

My jaw dropped. I hadn't expected this.

"I believe you learned to sew at Aston Hall," she continued. "And so I've got you a position, on a factory sewing line, making nightclothes. You start on Monday. You'll get the bus outside here. 7am prompt."

"Thank you," I mumbled.

Inside, I was bursting with excitement, but I was wary of showing it. If I appeared too pleased, she might well withdraw her offer.

The following Monday, as instructed, I was at the bus stop bright and early. The bus took me into the bus station in Derby city centre, and from there I was to get a second bus to the factory. As we pulled into the bus station, I saw the dreary little waiting room and had a sudden flashback to myself as a terrified 15-year-old, cowering in the corner of that same waiting room, pleading for someone to believe my story. I vividly remembered the cold of the plastic chairs against the back of my bare legs. I remembered my mother reading me the riot act after I got home. I remembered Miss Clark, her face devoid of emotion.

'This kind of thing doesn't happen in families… you are a sexual deviant…'

The bus jerked to a halt. We all got off and I found my connecting ride. It was thrilling being out in the world, making my own decisions. At last, I had somewhere to go. I wasn't stuck in a waiting room, daydreaming, any longer.

My heart raced as I walked into the factory and announced my name. Despite being excited, I was also visibly frightened and wary. It felt odd, having so much responsibility. Although I was 18 and had been through more trauma than the majority of adults, I was also in some ways terribly immature. Socially, I was stunted. I had no idea how to interact with other people. I didn't know how to look after myself either, I'd never paid a bill or cashed a cheque or taken responsibility for a dripping tap or a dodgy lock. I'd never had to make a decision or a basic choice, I'd never had to think for myself. Worse still, I had never been *allowed* to think for myself. Right down to the clothes I wore and the food I ate, it was all decided for me and I had to go along with it, like an obedient pet. My independence had been taken away, along with my sanity, my dignity and my self-esteem.

At the factory, nobody paid much attention to my wide eyes and trembling hands, and I was simply shown to a stool and told to sit down. I was one in a long line of workers; it was my job to sew on the sleeves, the next girl sewed the hems, the next did the patterns, and so on.

"You new here, love?" asked my workmates. "Where are you from then?"

They were all so friendly and welcoming, and even though I enjoyed their chatter, I was shy and kept myself pretty much to myself. The truth is, I was embarrassed of who I was and where I came from. I didn't want to have to tell them that I lived at a hostel, so I told them nothing.

But despite my reticence, there was a good atmosphere in the factory, and I grew to love my job. It was an escape, a total change of scene. For me, going to work was a little like going on holiday. I was paid £5 at the end of the week, and I had to pay my bus fare and give Miss Halliwell money for board, too. It didn't strike me as at all odd that I had to pay her for keeping me there against my will. It didn't occur to me, either, to ask where all the years of my child benefit had gone.

But luckily £5 went a long way in those days. I still had plenty left over to buy a bar of chocolate and a packet of cigarettes. I often picked up a small bar of Dairy Milk for Monica, and I even brought cigarettes back in for the other girls, who weren't allowed to leave the hostel, because of bad behaviour. They tried to persuade me to steal for them, too, to bring back goodies or new clothes. But I flatly refused. I didn't want to take any risks. Each morning on my way to work, Miss Halliwell would give me a packed lunch of sandwiches, fruit, and maybe some leftovers from the previous meal. Often the sandwiches were fish paste. Just the smell of the stuff turned my stomach and, after sniffing the bag, I would simply stash it under the bus seat if it smelled at all fishy. One day, the bus driver caught me doing it and reported me to Miss Halliwell.

"How dare you throw away good food!" she boomed.

I shook my head in apology and promised her truthfully that it would never happen again.

"No packed lunches for a week," snapped Halliwell. "You can go hungry. See how you like that."

I was starving for the entire week. But it still didn't

persuade me to like fish paste. Throwing away fishy butties was the closest I came to breaking the rules. It just wasn't in me. I was making progress and I wanted to keep it that way.

My 19th birthday came in December 1972, and I was still at the hostel, still working in the factory, still following the rules. It was a stable and uneventful period of my life. Perhaps I would not go as far as to say I was happy, I had forgotten by that stage what happiness actually felt like. But maybe it was my version of happy. When the New Year of 1973 dawned, my thoughts drifted naturally to the future and to new beginnings. I didn't want to spend my entire life in the hostel. But neither did I want a partner or a family. The idea of a close relationship with anyone was abhorrent to me. I couldn't even sit next to a man, never mind live with one. The abuse had scared me and scarred me – and I did not see how that could ever change. Even so, I used to fantasise about having my own little flat, with my own set of keys, and my own front door. I wanted a normal life and I wanted to be free. Yet the notion of freedom terrified and excited me in equal measure.

Chapter Sixteen

At Christmas, we were allowed to put up a tree with decorations, and we had a party too, piling all the furniture into the corner of the dining room, switching off the lights and blasting out Christmas songs from the radio.

I loved watching the other girls dancing. But I never joined in. I found I couldn't let myself go; I couldn't enjoy that taste of happiness. Years of repression had made me wary and afraid.

"Come on, Carol," they laughed, as they danced to John Lennon's *Happy Xmas (War is Over)*.

But I shook my head and smiled. I was happy spectating. There was no Christmas card from my family and no suggestion that I might go home. But I told myself I wasn't bothered. I didn't want to go home, not if Ian was there. Besides, my parents never bothered much with presents or celebrations, so I figured I was better off at the hostel in many ways.

"Stuff them all," I said to myself, as I peeled the potatoes, ready for our Christmas dinner. "I don't need anyone."

Chapter Sixteen

I had been in Craigmore for just over a year when, one day early in 1973, I heard the doorbell. Only Miss Halliwell was allowed to answer the door and so I carried on with the jigsaw I was working on, surrounded by the other girls. But then, above the chatter, I heard Miss Halliwell's voice:

"No, you certainly cannot see Carol Mackie. You can't just turn up here unannounced."

My ears pricked up at the sound of my name. And then, unmistakeably, a voice which ought to have been balm to my troubled soul, but which instead sent a shiver of dread through me.

"She's my daughter," shouted my mother. "I only want a quick word."

I froze. The jigsaw pieces in front of me were swimming. I couldn't stop trembling. Despite myself, I ran to the front door, as though my legs had a mind of their own. Miss Halliwell turned and sighed.

"Now that you're here, you might as well see what your mother wants," she said. "Though I might add this is all highly improper."

My mother looked at me as though this was no big deal, as though perhaps we'd seen each other the previous day and she was just popping in to say hello. Her legs, I noticed, were heavily bandaged and she was wearing a long skirt, an old-fashioned, patterned coat, and a tatty pair of men's slippers which were dark at the toes where the damp had seeped through.

"What is it? What's happened?" I asked.

My mind was racing. For my mother to turn up out of the blue, it had to be serious. Had something happened to one of my sisters? Or to my dad? Maybe it was Peter – had he been hit by a car? A range of accidents and tragedies whirred through my mind. It seemed an age before she spoke, then when she did her voice was plaintive, pleading. But her eyes were beady and cold.

"Thing is, we've no money at home, no money to feed the children," she said, without a hint of embarrassment. "Can you help, Carol? Can you help your little sisters?"

She was on her way to bingo, that was why she wanted money. I knew her too well. I wanted to yell at her, to shake her, to expose her for the hopeless, callous, mean-spirited cow that she was. Even for her, this was rich. She had not bothered with me for so many years. On my visit home, from Aston Hall, she had made it clear that I was not welcome. She had never so much as sent me a birthday card. And now – when she had probably got wind of me earning a wage – she was here to ask for my money. Even then, she could not be honest and tell me she wanted to spend it at bingo. She had to use my young sisters as emotional blackmail. Luckily, Miss Halliwell came to my rescue, because I found I could not reply.

"Absolutely not," she said firmly. "You must not come here and please don't ask Carol for money again. It's her money, not yours."

And with that, she closed the door on my mother and I crumpled with relief. Miss Halliwell's hypocrisy was not lost on me. She was the one who took away most of my weekly wage. But at that moment, I was grateful to her. I felt that she was on my side, that I had someone fighting my corner, if only for that brief moment. I went back to my jigsaw, but I struggled to concentrate. As much as I told myself I didn't care about my mother, as much as I tried to convince myself I was impervious to pain, I felt wounded. She was my mother. The one person who was supposed to love and protect me, to cherish and nurture me. Yet for some reason, she hated me. Worse still, I did not know why.

*****

With the spring of 1973 came an announcement that was to change my life. Miss Halliwell called me into the office for what would be the last time ever.

"You will leave the hostel next week," she informed me. "Your job at the factory will finish the day before you leave here. It's time, Carol. It's time to make your own way in the world."

I felt a rush of excitement, closely followed by dread. All alone, at last. I had wanted and feared this for so long. Now that it was coming, I didn't really know what to do.

The big day dawned and, just as Aston Hall, it took me no more than a few moments to pack my belongings.

I had little idea where I was going next, or what it would be like.

"It'll be a council flat," one of the girls predicted. "Old Halliwell will have sorted it out."

"I reckon she's going to another halfway house, bit like this, only not so strict," said another.

The truth was, none of us really knew. After breakfast, I said my goodbyes to the girls. Monica and I made jokes, both trying to put a brave face on things. But I knew I would miss her terribly. I fought back tears as I reached the top of the landing and the girls all gathered to wave me off. I allowed myself a half turn over my shoulder as I walked down the staircase, and I saw Monica's eyes, shining with tears, her face crumpled in distress. It tore at my heartstrings. But I couldn't fall apart, not now. And so I faced forward, with my head held high, dignified and defiant.

Downstairs, Miss Halliwell showed me to the front door, opened it and said:

"Good luck, Carol. Be a good girl."

I peered outside. There was no car waiting. No sign of Miss Clark. No sign of my dad. No instructions, no directions, no forward plan.

"Off you go," she said, a little impatiently.

"Where?" I asked, screwing my face up in confusion. "Go where?"

Miss Halliwell gave me a blank look.

"That's up to you," she said.

And with that, she gave me a little tap on the shoulder. I walked forward and the door clanged shut behind me, for the last time. I stared around me, at the road, the houses, at the big wide world. It seemed suddenly very intimidating. Usually, I loved the feeling of sunshine and fresh air on my face. But now, all I wanted to do was run back indoors. I needed the comfort of rules and regulations. Perversely, I craved the imprisonment and the punishment.

What was I supposed to do?

I had nowhere to go, nobody to rely on. The thought of sleeping rough was terrifying and I didn't even have so much as a blanket. In despair, I found a 2p coin in my purse and walked to the nearest phonebox. I had a sinking feeling as I dialled my home number. But I felt I had no other choice. To my relief, it was my dad who answered.

"I have nowhere to go," I said miserably. "Can I come home?"

"Where are you?" he asked.

"Burton Road," I replied, my heart lifting a little.

"I'm on my way," he said.

When I put the phone down, I burst into tears. I was grateful to Dad, despite everything. But I was frightened and nervous – angry and confused, too. I was very mixed up. But one thing was for certain, I knew that going home was not the answer to my problems. In spite of all my misgivings, I felt a little thrill when I saw Dad's work van driving down the road towards me.

"Hop in," he smiled. "Let's get you home."

I hadn't seen him for 18 months and he looked much older and wearier than I remembered.

"You're all grown up," he remarked. "I'd hardly have recognised you."

We drove on in silence and, just before we reached the top of our street, I mustered all my courage and asked: "Is Ian still at home?"

Dad waited a beat before he answered.

"Oh no," he replied. "He left over a year ago now, love. We had a falling out. You'll be able to have your old room back, sharing of course, but the girls will be pleased to see you."

An image of my old bedroom, with Ian's bunk beds lurking next door, flared in my mind and I found myself struggling to breathe. It was though something was crushing my lungs, as though he was pinning me down, once again.

"Your mother's at bingo," Dad added, as he pulled on the handbrake. "So a bit of peace, eh?"

He winked and I smiled. It felt good to be with my dad again. And I couldn't wait to see Ava and the twins. I'd missed them so much, though I'd never allowed myself to admit it until now.

"You're back!" they squealed, throwing their arms around me.

Everyone had changed; grown taller and older. One of the twins had put on some weight. Little Steven was all grown up and had taken to wearing a suit every day! Ava was full of news.

"Hey, you'll never believe this," she said. "Ian has moved in with his girlfriend. They've got a baby themselves."

My jaw went slack and I felt sick.

"What's the matter with you?" she asked.

"Nothing," I mumbled. "Nothing at all."

The thought of Ian having children of his own sent a chill through me. And yet, what could I do about it? I had tried to confide in my mother, in the social workers, in Dr Milner. I had told the truth. But nobody would listen. The only person who had truly listened and truly believed me, was Sandy. And as an image of her kind face floated into in my mind, I felt a spasm of worry. I wondered how she was getting on, and whether she was still stuck in Aston Hall.

"Wherever you are, I hope you're OK, Sandy," I whispered.

Mum arrived home late that night and paid me no attention whatsoever. But that was just as I expected.

"You'll pay board and lodgings whilst you're here," she said, without even making eye contact.

She even made me hand over almost £20, which I had saved from my sewing job at the factory.

Over the next few days, although everyone was more grown up, I learned that not much had changed at all at home. There were still 11 of us, crammed into that tiny house. Mum and Dad now slept in the living room on a pull-down bed which doubled as a wardrobe during the day. I had been used to so much space, calm and quiet. But this place was all clutter and chaos. I had left the psychiatric hospital behind. But at home, conversely, I felt like I was stuck in a madhouse.

"Can't you turn the bloody music down?" I yelled, as a din pounded through the bedroom floor.

I noticed the dirt – and the stench, too. The place was filthy. I almost hankered after the bleachy, sterile smells of Aston Hall and Craigmore. And just as before, Mum did little housework. It was left to me and my sisters to divide the tasks up between us. That was nothing new. But it itched, like a scab that would not heal, and fuelled my resentment and hatred of her. I knew she didn't want me at home. And I was determined not to be there any longer than was absolutely necessary.

I felt as though, in addition to Mum's original dislike of me, my presence now served as a constant and unwelcome reminder of the events of the past four years and the mistakes they had made. Every time one of my siblings mentioned Aston Hall or Craigmore Hostel, either one of my parents would quickly interject to shut the conversation down, in a way that made me think they were terrified of what I might say.

"So, what did you do in the hostel, Carol?" Ava asked. "Did you have a job? Did you make any friends? And do you miss it? Do you wish you could go back?"

"I don't think we need to talk about that," Dad would say. "It's all behind us now."

Or Mum would butt in, "Less of that! I don't want to hear it!"

They both seemed to think that by ignoring the past, we could pretend it had never happened and simply brush it all away. I suspect their motives for doing so, however, were completely different. Dad, I think, felt a crippling sense of shame and guilt. But Mum was bored by the whole topic. It irritated her when I was the centre of attention, for whatever the reason. But the end result was the same. I was forced to bury the abuse, deeper and deeper. I was not allowed to talk about Dr Milner, or the truth drug, or the gauze mask over my face. Why did nobody want to hear it? Perhaps it had all been my fault. Perhaps I had brought all this on myself, just as I had caused the abuse from Ian. And now, I was like a rotten smell, evoking unpleasant memories, spoiling the mood.

The same week after leaving Craigmore, I went to the Job Centre and got a job in a biscuit factory. I was on a line, packing biscuits along with hundreds of other girls. It was noisy there, too, but it was organised and, most importantly, it was clean. I loved it. I made lots of friends and at break time, we'd giggle and gossip over cigarettes and nibble the bits of broken biscuits we'd salvaged from the bins. I earned £19 a week and Mum demanded my entire wage, whining that she didn't have enough money to feed the family. Somehow, of course, she always had enough money for bingo, but not enough time to find a job herself. I squirrelled away as much money as I could, but it just about covered my bus fare, my cigarettes and my packed lunches.

"I'll never be able to save up and leave this place at this rate," I told Ava miserably. "I'll be stuck here with the old cow forever."

"You might even end up playing bingo every day," Ava said, and for some reason, we both found her prediction impossibly funny, and we laughed until the tears rolled down our cheeks.

During one break, I found myself standing next to a young Asian bloke. His name was Ahmed, and he worked on the ovens.

"I could give you a lift home after your shift," he offered. "Save you getting the bus? I think you live near me."

I gawped. I'd never been in a car with a strange man before. I still found it nerve-racking sitting next to my own father, never mind a complete stranger.

"Go on," he smiled, sensing my indecision. "I won't bite, I promise you. It's a foul day as well, it'll save you waiting at the bus stop for ages."

I nodded, uncertainly, and instantly regretted it. But the journey home was nothing like as traumatic as I'd feared. Ahmed made polite conversation and arranged to pick me up, the following morning, for work. For a couple of weeks, that was our pattern. But one day, as I opened the front door, I heard one of my younger sisters shouting.

"Mum! Mum! Our Carol has just got out of a Pakistani's car! She's going out with a Pakistani!"

I froze. I knew I was in for trouble. Sure enough, seconds later, my mother hobbled angrily into the hallway, lightning quick despite her bandaged leg.

"What the hell do you think you're playing at?" she growled. "Don't ever bring a Paki to this door or this estate. Understood?"

Silently, I was screaming at her. But outwardly, I simply shrugged. I had no other choice.

"I just got a lift home," I replied. "That was all."

"Well, don't do it again!" she rasped.

I nodded meekly, but the next day, after work, I climbed into Ahmed's car with a smile. Now that my mother had forbidden me, I had to do it.

"Just drop me at the top of our estate," I said to him. "I can walk the last part."

He didn't question why, and I was too mortified to explain. For another few days, the lifts continued, with Ahmed and I chatting politely each day on our journey. He seemed like the perfect gentleman. But then, one afternoon, he said:

"It's a nice day, let's go for a drive before I take you home."

My only sexual experiences to date had been at the

depraved hands of my brother and Dr Milner. In my mind, sex went hand in hand with abuse and pain. I had never even kissed a boy and had no experience of being in their company to judge the good from the bad. But, working in factories, listening to the exploits of the other girls, I was hardly naïve about what went on, either. I knew exactly what he had in mind. He was a good-looking young man, although I didn't fancy him, and I certainly didn't want to have sex with him. But I also knew that it was a hurdle in life I had to overcome. I had to tick it off my list – no more than that. Ahmed seemed like a nice bloke, After all, if not him, then who else?

I lost my virginity in the car, that same day. It was over mercifully fast and I didn't enjoy it at all. Afterwards, as always, I had to ask Ahmed to drop me off at the top of our estate. It struck me as completely warped that my own brother had been allowed to sexually abuse me, under the same roof, for years. And yet my first boyfriend was not even allowed near our house, because of the colour of his skin.

Three weeks later, in September 1973, I missed a period. I was panic-stricken.

"Can you get pregnant on your first time?" I asked the girls at work. "I thought it took months?"

There were a few sniggers and a murmur of sympathy.

"Carol, did you not use protection? A condom? Nothing? You silly thing."

I shook my head. I didn't even know what condoms were. Now, it seemed a bit too late to find out. At home, panic coursing through me, I broke the news to my mother. She shot me a look of pure contempt.

"Is it the Paki's?" she demanded.

I nodded.

"I might not even be pregnant," I said desperately, even though I felt sick and my breasts were tender. "I need a test."

"You need to see the doctor," she said. "But you'd better not be bloody pregnant, not with his baby."

She stalked past me, giving me a wide berth, as though I had a disease she could catch. I squirmed. It wasn't me having a baby that worried her. It was me having a baby with a different colour of skin. I knew, deep down, that the test would be positive. Later that same week, as we sat in the surgery, the news was confirmed.

"She doesn't want to keep it," Mum told the GP, over my shoulder. "She's going to get rid of it."

But I fancied I could already feel the fluttering of new life inside me, and I had no intention of having a termination. I'd expected to be devastated at the news that I was pregnant. Instead, I found I was secretly rather thrilled.

"No way," I said. "I'll do what I want."

The next day at work, I waited for a moment to get Ahmed on his own. With him on my side, I felt sure I'd be fine. Together, we'd show my parents how wrong they were. Outside, as we shivered our way through our break, I pulled him aside.

"Listen," I whispered. "I'm having a baby. I've had a test."

Ahmed's face dropped.

"How do you know it's mine?" he said, shiftily.

I was furious. This wasn't what I had expected at all.

"How dare you?" I whispered, struggling to keep my voice down. "I've had sex once and once only and it was with you. Of course it's your baby.

"And I'll tell you another thing – I'm keeping it."

I was shaking with anger and indignation when I made my way back inside to the production line. Tears streamed down my cheeks as I packed ginger nuts and custard creams.

"Carol," whispered one of my pals. "I know it's none of my business, duck. But Ahmed is married. Did you know?"

In shock, I leaned forward onto the emergency stop button, and the whole conveyor belt juddered to a halt. All the biscuits piled up and fell off the end of the belt, onto the floor.

"What's going on?" yelled the supervisor.

I ran to the toilet, with my heart racing.

"Sod him," I muttered to myself. "Don't need him. Don't need anyone."

The odds were stacked against me, but that was nothing new and despite everything, I couldn't help feeling pleased.

I was having a baby. A beautiful, innocent, precious new life. This was a new start and I would grasp it with both hands.

When I arrived home that afternoon, there was a social worker waiting. She and Mum sat in the living room, sipping tea, like the execution committee. I shot Mum a thunderous look. I knew this was her doing.

"Your mother tells me you're pregnant, Carol," said the social worker.

"It's got nothing to do with you," I retorted.

"I'm afraid that's where you're wrong," she said. "You're not yet capable of coping on your own."

I sighed in frustration.

"I can cope perfectly well," I spat. "I've got a job, I'm looking for a new place to live. It's none of your business what I do."

The social worker pursed her lips tightly and she and my mother exchanged glances. I knew this wasn't the last of it, but I was determined to fight them all the way.

Six months into my pregnancy, I was blossoming. I barely had a bump, and I felt full of hope.

"You're a little pea in a pod," I said gently, a hand on my belly. "Mummy loves you."

I had said nothing to my bosses at the factory because I wanted to continue working for as long as possible. Late one afternoon as I walked home, a car screeched to a halt beside me and Ahmed sprang out and grabbed hold of me. Before I could scream, he had clamped one hand over my mouth and began whipping me, repeatedly, with what looked like an old flex lead from a kettle.

"You're a little whore," he hissed. "Stop telling people it's my baby. My wife will find out. Keep your mouth shut."

The pain shot through me and, as I sank to the tarmac, all I could think of was my poor baby. Had she been hurt? Had she even survived? I could hear cars passing, there was even someone on foot on the side of the road, but nobody stopped to help. I realised they were probably more horrified by the fact that a man of colour was on our estate, rather than by the actual attack.

Ahmed left me lying on the pavement. After he had gone, I limped home, bloodied and bruised. Dad took one look at me and called the police. The officers came out and took photos. Ahmed was arrested.

I went to hospital for checks and the baby, thankfully, was unharmed. For days, I had painful red weals all across my back, but they didn't worry me. I had been through far worse, after all. Ahmed was later jailed for 18 months, but to me, it felt like he had got away lightly.

Towards the end of the pregnancy, we had another visit from social services. I was upstairs resting my swollen ankles after an early shift at work, when I overheard voices.

"She's not fit to look after a baby and we won't do it," my mother was saying. "We want no part of it. I don't want her or her baby here."

"I quite agree," the social worker was saying. "I see your point of view."

My heart was heavy. I knew I couldn't rely on my parents, not at the moment. But I could only hope that, when the time came, they might relent. Surely, when they met their grandchild, they would reconsider. Or perhaps the social worker could find me a place, a mother and baby unit or maybe even my own flat. I would do anything – anything – to keep my baby.

In the early hours one morning in April 1974, I woke with unbearable back pain. I took two paracetamol and tried to go back to sleep, but it was impossible. By morning, my contractions were starting, irregular at first and still quite weak, but I knew this was it. With a mixture of excitement and panic, I packed a little overnight bag and counted out my bus fare. Dad's van was parked outside. But I knew there was no point in asking for a lift. Downstairs, Ava was already up, mooching around the kitchen in her dressing-gown.

"Carol!" she gasped, when she saw my white face. "What's up? Has it started?"

I nodded, gripping the kitchen work surface as another contraction took hold.

"Shall I come to the hospital with you?" she said. "Hold your hand?"

I was about to nod, gratefully, when my mother's words hit us like bullets from the upstairs landing.

"You can go on your own!" she yelled. "That will teach you."

Ava looked at me apologetically. She didn't dare defy our mother and I understood. So, carrying nothing more than a nightie and a change of underwear, I caught two buses to The Queen Mary Hospital, Derby, biting my lip as the contractions came stronger and harder. By the time I got to the maternity unit I could hardly walk. And on the labour ward, as the pain grew worse still, I screamed in agony. It seemed to go on forever.

"I can't do this!" I sobbed. "I really can't!"

It was so lonely, without anyone to squeeze my hand or give me reassurance. The midwives did their best, but it wasn't the same as having my sister with me. And hearing happy couples around me, proud dads and fussing grandparents, just made it so much worse. Why was I on my own?

Eight hours on, my baby daughter was laid in my arms. The most beautiful little bundle I had ever seen. She had masses of jet black hair, flawless olive skin, and the biggest, liquid brown eyes. I named her Jasmine. I cuddled her close, drinking her in. Surely, surely, when my parents saw her, they too would love her?

"Can you call my parents and ask them to visit?" I asked a nurse.

I felt the request might be better coming from the staff. She nodded, kindly, but didn't reply. I had the uneasy feeling that she knew something I didn't. But I was too afraid of asking questions, because, deep down, I knew I didn't want to hear the answers.

I didn't have a single item of baby clothing, so the nurses gave me clothes and blankets, and I bathed and dressed my little girl. For 10, glorious days, Jasmine and I lived in a precious bubble. We were in a private room, just the two of us. I cared for her all on my own, knowing that each minute with her was a privilege and an honour, but fearing that at any moment she might be taken away.

"I love you," I told her over and over. "I love you and I always will."

There were so many promises I wanted to make, but I was worried I might not be able to keep them. As the days passed, a glimmer of hope built and burned inside me, despite myself. Perhaps they had changed their minds? Maybe I would be allowed to keep her after all?

They hadn't visited, nobody had. But maybe they were waiting to meet her at home. Each night, I lay awake, desperate not to waste any time sleeping, instead staring at my perfect little daughter, memorising her tiny, button nose and her chubby little hands.

"Please," I begged silently. "Please don't let them take her away."

On the tenth day, two social workers arrived. One went straight to Jasmine's cot, the other came to my bedside.

"It's time now," she said, as though she was announcing

the start of a TV programme. "It's time for us to take the baby."

For a moment, I didn't react. I let the words wash past me, not wanting to believe it was true. I had known this day had to come and yet, now it was here, it seemed appallingly cruel and unjust. I had looked after my little girl, single-handedly, for 10 days. I had fed and winded her, I had done the night feeds, I had changed her nappies. I had proved that I could cope. I had proved myself as much as any other first-time mother.

"Please," I said, in a voice so quiet I could barely hear it myself. "Can I keep her? Can you help me?"

The social worker shook her head, brisk and business-like. Her colleague was already scooping Jasmine into a blanket, ready to leave.

I simply stared, frozen, immobilised with horror. To my shame, I did not shout, or scream or even object. I look back on that moment now and I do not understand why I didn't throw myself against the door, claw out their eyes and beat them with my bare hands, to try to save my baby daughter.

My only reasoning is that I had no belief in myself. I had no power and no worth. Years of abuse, years of suffering, had taught me that my opinion did not matter a jot. I knew they would win. Always. So what was the point?

As Jasmine left the room, I felt the breath being sucked out of me. I sat motionless, staring at her empty cot, with a pain in my heart so sharp that each breath was shallow and short. Eventually, a nurse walked past the door.

"You can go home now," she said. "Get your stuff packed, love. We'll need this bed for another patient shortly."

Like a robot, I walked out of the hospital, with my arms aching to hold my daughter, with my heart longing to feel that love again. I'd had her for just 10 days, yet she had transformed my life. I was a mother now. Nothing could ever change that. But I was a mother without a child. I missed her so much, it was agony.

Nobody came to collect me. I got one bus, then the other, home by myself. At home, I let myself in and slipped into the front room, where I laid my head on the table and wept. Mum was at home, I could hear her bustling about the house. Dad was at work. Later in the day, Ava came home and put her arm around me.

"I'm really sorry," she said softly. "I can't think what you must be feeling."

For the next two weeks, life was a horrible blur. I hardly ate. I didn't wash and I didn't get dressed. Apart from Ava, nobody even bothered to ask how I was. In my parents' opinion, I had brought this on myself and this was my punishment. I had got my just desserts. I had nothing to remind me of Jasmine, no photos, no keepsakes, not even a little bootee. But nothing would ever erase the memories of those few days we had shared. I had those, at least.

"Whoever adopts her, please love her," I pleaded. "Make her happy."

The social worker visited again with the final paperwork, and I listened, dully, as she told me how my daughter would have a much better life without me.

"Her new mother runs a cafe," she told me. "She's going to be very happy with her new family. You must not look for her. You are not allowed to contact her or communicate with her in any way."

Her words felt like a knife running through me. She might as well have ripped out my heart. Always, throughout my life, whatever happened to me I managed to stay positive. Even when Ian was abusing me, even during the drugged up, messed up days at Aston Hall I had found some lightness, even humour. But now, with my baby gone, I had reached rock bottom. I felt completely defeated and broken. My nervous tics became worse. I pulled neurotically at my fingers and nodded my head in a desperate, pointless rhythm. I had always hated my mother, but now, I loathed her with a passion. In my mind, rightly or wrongly, she was at the centre of all my misery and I wanted nothing more to do with my family. Their cruelty towards me felt unforgivable.

As the fog of my grief lifted slightly, I realised with a sudden and painful clarity that I had to get out of the house. And this time, it would be for good. It felt like an impossible challenge. I had no money for a place of my own because Mum had taken every penny of wages from me. And I had lost my job, too, whilst I was having my baby. In desperation, I went to see a friend, Cara She was from the local neighbourhood.

"Please can I stay for a while?" I asked. "I'll sleep on the couch. I'll get a job and pay board."

She nodded kindly.

"Course you can," she smiled. "Come in, Carol, you look bloody awful. You poor girl."

I was not used to sympathy and I burst into floods of tears, right there and then, on her doorstep. It had got to the stage where I didn't even feel I deserved a few kind words.

Later that day, I went to the Job Centre and got a job at the bus station cafe, starting that same week. It felt oddly familiar walking back into the bus station, with the ghost of my teenage self still sitting in the aptly-named waiting room, still hoping for someone to believe my story. If I had known what anguish lay in wait for me, perhaps I would have run away even further. Yes, perhaps I would have run right out of Derby and never looked back.

Chapter Seventeen

In the weeks that followed, without my family around me, I began to feel better. In the evenings, Cara dragged me out around the pubs and clubs of Derby.

"It'll do you good, Carol," she insisted.

And she was right. Together, we knocked back Bacardis and stayed out until 2am, before getting up for work at 6am, groggy and hungover. It was nice to be young and silly for a change. But I was never carefree. Jasmine was never far from my mind. Cara and all the other girls in the group had boyfriends. But it just wasn't for me. That one encounter with Ahmed and the tragedy which followed had been enough to confirm that I had no interest at all in love or sex. Ian and Dr Milner truly had put me off the idea of relationships for the rest of my life.

"Come on, Carol, just let your hair down," Cara persuaded. "One date won't kill you. You might even have fun. You don't have to sleep with anyone if you don't fancy it. Just enjoy yourself."

But I couldn't be talked round. I was resolutely single

and unapproachable, I became well-known for it. Then one night, in a local pub, I got talking to a man called Sunny Minto. His real name was William George Minto, and he was 17 years older than me. He was gorgeous – 5'10" and well built, rippling with muscles. He was casually dressed in jeans and a jacket, but he looked clean and sharp.

"Can I buy you a drink?" he asked.

I shook my head, doubtfully. I fancied him and I got on well with him, but I just didn't want to get involved.

"Please?" he persisted.

But I shook my head, more firmly this time. Over the next year, Sunny and I became really good friends. I learned that he was a widower. Originally from a rural area of Jamaica, Boscobel in St Mary's Parish, he had come to England as part of the Windrush generation, and he'd had more than his fair share of heartbreak, just as I had. Sunny was quiet and unassuming, and a good, decent man, who worked hard in a cable factory. Though he liked a lager and black, or an occasional Jack Daniels, he wasn't a big drinker or a hell-raiser. He wanted a relationship and, deep down, I slowly realised that I did too. Every few weeks he would ask me out on a date. I wanted to say yes, but I didn't know how. I just couldn't put the past behind me.

"He'd be perfect for you," Cara told me. "He adores you, everyone can see that."

I knew she was right. Yet still, I held on. One Saturday

night, around three years after I'd first met Sunny, I went to the pub as usual.

"Where's Sunny?" I asked, noticing straightaway that he was missing.

"Oh, he's got a new girlfriend, apparently," said one of my pals. "He'll be staying at home, doing you know what!"

Suddenly, my drink turned bitter in my mouth. The thought of Sunny with another woman left me reeling. Without another word, I plonked my glass down, grabbed my coat, and left. It wasn't far to Sunny's flat and I marched all the way there, with my cheeks burning. How could I have been so foolish to let such a good man slip through my fingers? From somewhere, I found a confidence I never knew I had and I banged on his door like I owned the place. Sunny answered and let me in without saying a word. In the living room, sitting on the couch, was his new girlfriend. What I said next amazed me – I hadn't been planning it at all.

"I think you'd better be going," I told her. "And don't come back."

She looked at Sunny, who said nothing, but nodded, slightly. As she flounced out, a slow smile spread across his face until he was beaming, from ear to ear. From that night, we were never apart. After our first kiss, all my hang ups about men, sex and relationships simply dissolved. Sunny was my soulmate, I knew that for certain.

"We should have no secrets," he told me. "I want you to tell me everything."

"You might regret saying that," I told him with a wry smile.

Where to start? But strangely, I found Sunny so easy to confide in. It all came spilling out: Ian, Dr Milner, Jasmine. One heartbreaking trauma after another.

"Wow," he said, when I had eventually finished. "Carol, you've been through some shit."

After sharing my secrets, I felt somehow lighter and brighter, as though Sunny was sharing my load. With his arms around me, I felt safe. He was at once strong and powerful, yet incredibly gentle and humane. With Sunny on my side, I felt I could do anything. And he wasn't just a shoulder to cry on. He wanted to help and tackle each of my problems, one by one.

"Let's bring Jasmine here to live with us," he suggested. "I'll support you. We could apply to adopt her."

I shook my head miserably.

"The adoption was finalised years ago and I'm not allowed any contact. I don't know where she is or even what her name is now. It wouldn't be fair to steamroller our way into her new life and take her away from the people she thinks are her parents."

"What about Ian then? Give me his address," he demanded. "I'm going to see him."

I hadn't seen Ian since coming out of Craigmore Hostel. In fact, I hadn't seen him since that brief visit home, from Aston Hall, when I was 18. But I knew where he lived. I was still in touch with Ava and she gave me news of the family from time to time.

"Don't do anything silly," I pleaded. "I don't want you to get into any trouble."

"I'll be fine," Sunny promised.

At home, I waited on tenterhooks, hoping Sunny would keep his temper. When I heard his key in the door later, I ran into the hallway and threw my arms around him.

"Don't worry, I didn't lay a finger on him. I just told him exactly what I thought of him," he told me. "He won't be bothering you ever again."

I tried to act as though I was used to having handsome men fight my corner, but inside, I was bursting with pride and joy. At last, I had someone to stand up for me, someone on my side. In short, I had someone who loved me. And it felt fantastic.

"You should stand up for yourself, Carol," Sunny told me. "I'm right behind you. Always remember that. We're a team now."

Me and Sunny settled into a happy routine. We bought our own home, a three-bedroom Victorian terraced house, with a beautiful bay window and a little garden. We had only been together a couple of months when I fell pregnant, and we were overjoyed. Memories of my first pregnancy came rushing back, but I knew this time was different. Nobody could take this baby away. I began planning for our new arrival, buying baby clothes and a cot.

But just before my 12-week scan, I began to bleed. Sunny rushed me to hospital, but a doctor confirmed I had miscarried. Together, we cried. But it made us all the more determined to try again. I fell pregnant a couple of months on, and this time, we were a little more cautious. Yet again, 10 weeks into the pregnancy, I was bent double with cramps and I began to bleed. After another dash to the hospital, our worst fears were confirmed.

"Why is this happening to me?" I wept.

It felt like a punishment, for failing Jasmine. Perhaps, as my mother had said, I was just a bad lot and everything was my fault. It was my fault Ian had abused me, my fault I'd gone to Aston Hall, my fault my baby had been taken away. And now, someone, somewhere, was making me pay. Over the next 18 months, I suffered a further six miscarriages. With each one, the pain just got worse.

"Let's go on holiday," Sunny suggested. "We need to take our minds off babies for a while."

We booked a trip to Jamaica, to see Sunny's family. I was so excited. I had never been abroad before. We both booked six weeks off work – all our annual leave in one go. Driving all the way to Heathrow in Sunny's car, a bright green Ford Escort, I felt like I was embarking on the biggest adventure of my life. Sunny's family lived on a farm deep in the Jamaican countryside and they grew passion fruit, coconuts, bananas, oranges and nutmeg. But conditions were basic and there wasn't even an inside toilet.

"You'd better get me back to Derby!" I joked.

Sunny was one of six children, and we stayed with his brother, Kalib, who was blind. The house was on an old plantation, isolated and dilapidated, and around two miles from the next dwelling. With an old wooden porch, stone floors and netting at the window frames, it was quaint but uncomfortable.

Like Sunny, Kalib was easy-going and laidback. The sun was unbearably hot, and it felt as though the mosquitos were eating me for breakfast, but the holiday was wonderful. Sunny's parents had both passed away, but I loved meeting the rest of his family and seeing the place where he'd grown up. He showed me the path he'd walked to school as a kid.

"We used to play for hours in these fields," he told me, with a nostalgic smile.

The six weeks flew by and all too soon, it was time to return home.

"That holiday was just what we needed," I said to Sunny, as we boarded the plane home. "I feel so relaxed."

One night, soon after we returned from Jamaica, Sunny turned to me and said nervously:

"Would you like to get married, Carol?"

I beamed and kissed him.

"I'm not exactly going anywhere am I?" I replied laughing. "Course I'll marry you."

In one way the proposal was completely unexpected, we had just been sitting at home, watching TV. But in another way, it was a natural step. Sunny and I belonged together. We were married at Derby register office in the summer of 1979. Ava attended and Sunny's best friend was best man. Afterwards, we had a meal at a local restaurant. It was a quiet day, but such a happy one.

Over the spring of 1980, I fell pregnant again. This time, I didn't even dare to hope. By now, I was 26 years old and I longed for a baby. Around me, friends were falling pregnant and I wished so much it could be me, too.

"This might be our lucky chance," Sunny smiled. "Let's just wait and see."

Incredibly, I reached the all-important 12 weeks without a problem. The weeks turned into months, and I blossomed. Sunny cooked me fried chicken and dumplings and delicious soups. Our son Karl was born in December 1980, weighing 5lbs 1oz. Sunny held my hand and urged me on, all through the labour. Baby Karl was the double of his daddy.

"He looks like he fell right out of your pocket," I beamed.

We took our little boy home, and I was on cloud nine. I had never believed such happiness was possible.

When Karl was three weeks old, I decided to take him to visit my family. Deep down, I knew there was a risk that they would reject us both. But he was so gorgeous and so innocent, I managed to convince myself that they would fall in love with him, just as I had. And despite all the wrongs of the past, I wanted Karl to have grandparents and aunts. I wanted a family – for him.

"Perhaps this can be a new start," I said to Sunny, as I packed a changing bag and tucked Karl into the pram.

It was just a few days before Christmas, too, so surely they would welcome us in? When I arrived at the house, the place was the usual bustle of activity and noise. Everyone was home. I knew Ian had moved out, so I had no concerns there.

"Ooh, it's Carol with the baby!" squealed one of my sisters, as she answered the door. "Look at his curly hair! Oh, what a little darling he is."

She took him into the kitchen and they all passed him round like he was a precious little parcel, and I beamed with pride.

"Here, let me take him into the living room to see Mum and Dad," I said.

They were both sitting on the couch but, as I walked in, cradling my son, Mum looked straight at him, stared for a second, and then very deliberately turned her head away. A split second later, Dad did the same thing. He at least had the decency to look a little uncomfortable and awkward. Mum simply looked bored. For a moment I stood in the doorway, uncertain, my lip trembling. I had left myself wide open by coming here and they knew it.

The rejection – so cold and so blatant – was hard to take. I marched out of the house with as much dignity as I could muster, with my face stinging, as though I had been slapped.

"Don't worry darling," I whispered, as I trundled the pram through the once-familiar streets of the estate. "We don't need them. Stuff 'em."

But there was no denying I was terribly hurt. Embarrassed, too. I felt foolish, more than anything, for giving my parents a second chance that they neither merited nor appreciated. I should have known that they would throw it right back at me. I didn't know whether their disapproval stemmed from Karl's heritage - I knew how prejudiced they had been when I was pregnant with Jasmine. Or perhaps their dislike was simply an extension of their feelings towards me. They hated me. They hated my son. I would never truly know the reasons behind their hostility, and I certainly would never understand. But one thing was for sure, I would not give them the opportunity to humiliate us again.

I pushed the incident from my mind, told myself I had no family, and concentrated instead on my wonderful husband and son. There was so much love, inside our four walls, that I needed to look no further.

Sunny worked hard every day and, in time, I went back to the biscuit factory on a twilight evening shift, 5pm – 10pm, so that we could look after Karl between us. Ava worked at the biscuit factory now, too, and she and I became closer than ever. Everything was perfect. Karl cried almost constantly for the first few months of his life, but I didn't let that worry me. After all I had suffered, it felt like a true privilege to get up during the night – even with a screaming baby. I just felt incredibly lucky.

When Karl was about six months old, he picked up a respiratory infection which he couldn't shake. After trips to and from the GP, he was admitted to hospital for some checks. As the doctor examined him, he came across a Mongolian spot on the base of Karl's spine. It was a harmless birthmark, more commonly found on black skin.

"What's this?" the doctor demanded. "How did your son get this bruise?"

"That's not a bruise," I explained. "My son is of dual race. This is a perfectly normal birthmark."

But the doctor didn't believe me.

"I think we need to speak to social services," he said.

His words sent a chill through me. All at once, I was a frightened teenager again, quivering in front of Miss Clark, the social worker, at Derby bus station. I tried to focus on the doctor, but I knew I sounded scared and defensive.

"Please, no," I pleaded. "I'm telling the truth. I would never hurt my son."

He shook his head.

"Let's see what the social worker says," he replied.

But I felt helpless. I was told to leave Karl in hospital, go home and wait for a call. In floods of tears, I raced back and found Sunny, just arrived home from work.

"Where's Karl?" he asked. "What did the hospital say?"

When I told him what had happened, he was furious. He went straight to the hospital and demanded to speak to a paediatrician.

"You ought to know all about the Mongolian spot," he told them. "It's not uncommon at all. I'm taking my son home now and I don't expect any more resistance from you."

The hospital staff were full of apologies and we all left together soon after. But I couldn't help feeling that I'd let Karl down somehow. Why hadn't I been able to stand up to them, as Sunny had? As soon as social services were mentioned, I had turned to jelly. I had become that same compliant, obedient little girl I'd been at Aston Hall. I thought I had left her behind. But it seemed she was still lurking, still hovering. I had been determined that Karl's childhood would not be overshadowed in any way by my own suffering. But already, at just six months old, he was being tainted. The legacy of the abuse lived on.

"Don't worry about it," Sunny consoled me. "You're bound to feel nervous around doctors and social workers."

Soon, we put the incident at the hospital behind us and concentrated on enjoying our little boy. Even as a toddler, Karl loved music. We had a record player in our front room, which we called the parlour, and Sunny would play music while we danced and sang.

"He's a chip off the old block, alright," I smiled.

Sunny loved cooking for us, too; Karl wrinkled his nose every time Sunny did his speciality fish soup, but he wolfed down the chicken dishes. In time, Karl started school, which he loved and he made lots of friends. He wasn't allowed to play in the street, it was too dangerous and I worried about him. But at weekends, he and his pals would play football in a carpark behind our house. Or maybe I'd take him to the park, to feed the ducks. One day, as I was throwing stale bread, my wedding ring slipped off, into the murky depths of the duck pond, never to be seen again.

"Sorry, Sunny," I said sadly, when we got home. "I loved that ring."

But he enveloped me in a hug.

"We don't need a wedding ring to prove how much we love each other," he told me.

On rainy days, we'd stay at home, put the record player on and play dominoes. They were such happy times. Sunny and I never argued at all; we were good friends. After years of turmoil and conflict, it was lovely to have found someone I could just be myself with. Of course, we would have liked a little brother or sister for Karl. But the years passed, and it never happened.

When Karl was old enough, I told him about Jasmine, his older half-sister who he would never get to meet.

"She's here in my heart, and yours, too," I told him. "We must never forget her."

The mention of her name always evoked a sadness

in me. Yet, after all my miscarriages, we knew we were fortunate just to have Karl, and it made me love him all the more.

Occasionally, though less often these days, I would have flashbacks to the abuse. Sometimes, I might be washing the dishes, when a sharp reminder would suddenly stop me in my tracks. Perhaps it could be a kitchen utensil, similar to the ones Ian used. Or maybe I would be counting out the plates and dishes, ready for dinner, and I would be transported, in an instant, back to Aston Hall, back to the truth drug, the strait jacket, the bars on the windows. At night, I insisted that my bed was higher than the window, so that I could see outside. I bought such a deep mattress that we felt like royalty, perched on the top. Sunny laughed at first, thinking it was a funny quirk of character, until I explained that I couldn't stand the feeling of being pinned down, of being unable to escape. I had to be near to the window, in case I needed to jump.

"I won't ever let anyone hurt you again," he promised, folding his arms around me. "You mustn't worry, my love."

I trusted him completely, and yet the insecurity and fear was still there. Sometimes, when I was out shopping, or on my way to work, I would spot a greasy, dark head from behind, and my stomach would lurch violently.

"Is that him?" I wondered. "Is that Ian?"

Ian lived, I knew, on the other side of Derby and so there was little chance of me bumping into him in my neighbourhood. Even so, I had flashes of panic if I saw someone who looked like him from afar. Taking deep breaths, I would repeat Sunny's words in my head:

"I won't ever let anyone hurt you."

And soon, I was calm again. With Sunny on my side, I knew I could face anything. We were a formidable team. More than that, we were deliriously, wonderfully happy.

When Karl was 12 years old, Sunny started complaining of back pain. I thought maybe he had been overdoing things.

"You've probably pulled a muscle at work," I said.

But over the next few weeks, his backache got worse. Sunny was a typical man; he didn't like going to the doctor. But eventually, I insisted.

Sunny was sent for an X-ray, and it came back clear. But still the pain continued. Next, he was sent for a scan – this time, it showed that his right kidney wasn't functioning properly.

"Don't worry too much about it," I said to Sunny. "If the worst comes to the worst, you can live with one kidney. I've read about it. You can even have one of mine if you like!"

But more tests found a tumour inside his kidney, and it was cancerous.

"I'm sorry, but it's terminal," said his consultant. "We can't offer any treatment at all."

I was inconsolable. Sunny tried to be strong for me but I could see the fear in his eyes. By now, he was losing weight rapidly and becoming very weak. I concentrated on caring for him, looking after Karl and working full-time. I kept myself busy and in denial, I kept telling myself that Sunny would get better. He was such a strong man, after all. And there was no way he would leave me and Karl, he knew we needed him. Eventually, he was taken into hospital. I stopped working so that I could be with him all the time. Two weeks later, on February 21 1993, his breathing became laboured and his nurses warned us that he was nearly at the end. As I sat, holding his hand, he turned his head slowly towards me and whispered:

"Promise me Carol, that you won't let people walk all over you."

Blinded by tears, I nodded and kissed his cheek. I was by his side soon after when he passed away, aged 56. He had been such a solid, vibrant man and I found it incomprehensible that he could have died so young. That he could have left me. I felt angry; furious, that I was left behind. Terrified, too, of how I would cope without him. But mostly, I felt an overwhelming, paralysing grief. My love was gone.

At his funeral, we played Bob Marley's *No Woman No Cry*. Sunny was buried at Nottingham Road cemetery, near our home. As I threw a white rose into his grave, I felt my heart splintering and cracking into pieces. I couldn't imagine how life would continue after this. I couldn't imagine ever smiling again.

"Goodbye," I whispered. "And thank you, my love."

Chapter Eighteen

The days after losing Sunny were very dark. I kept going, for Karl's sake, but it was so hard. Each night, I would lay the table for three people. I cooked Sunny's favourite dishes as if I could somehow tempt him back home and back to life. I waited for the sound of his key in the door after work. All day long, I kidded myself that he might be coming home. I just could not accept that he was gone. Each night, after I'd cooked for Karl, I went to the graveyard, to talk to him.

"I miss you, Sunny," I said softly. "Why did you have to leave me? Who will look after us now?"

Karl missed him too. Sunny had been a good father, strict but loving. We were lonely, just the two of us, but I knew better than to reach out to my family. Apart from Ava, my family had never even met Sunny, and so I certainly didn't want them around now that he was dead. But Ava often called in, to keep an eye on me.

"I'm worried about you, Carol," she said. "You're losing weight and you never go out. You need to pull yourself together and look forwards. Think about Karl."

One night, she insisted on me going to bingo with her. I had always avoided the bingo hall, it reminded me of my mother. But Ava practically dragged me out of the house. She had arranged for Karl to spend time with her kids whilst I was out. It was all organised, and she was trying to do me a favour, so I could hardly back out.

"Ok, just for an hour," I agreed.

But as soon as we had sat down with our books, I saw my mother, shuffling towards me, with a disgruntled look on her face.

"Look," I whispered to Ava. "There she is. I don't believe it."

I hadn't visited Mum since that awful visit when Karl was a newborn. She had aged a lot since we'd last seen each other, but then, I imagined, so had I. Now, under the glare of the bright lights of the bingo hall, I had no choice but to be polite. She brought her books and her pen over to sit with us, as though this was something we did all the time and it was just a regular family night out. After the hour was up, I stood up and put my coat on.

"I'll be off now," I announced. "I need to get home for my Karl."

Mum didn't even look up from her card. She was too busy playing bingo to be bothered with me. But then, it had always been that way.

*****

Less than a year after Sunny's death, Karl and I moved to a new home. I hated leaving behind all our happy memories as a family, but I needed somewhere smaller and more affordable. Karl had been as swamped with grief as I had, and I hoped this might be a new start for us both.

"We'll never forget your dad," I said to him. "But he'd want us to be happy."

I couldn't afford to buy again and our new flat, rented from Derby council, was on the first floor of a three-storey block. We quickly settled in and got to know our neighbours. One day, on the communal stairs, I bumped into a young woman struggling with a pram. I noticed, as she passed, that she had a black eye and it looked painful. For some reason, the woman's face stuck in my mind. I didn't know why, but I felt really sorry for her – disproportionately so. Perhaps, I told myself, I was nostalgic for that time in my own life, when Karl had been a baby in a pram and Sunny and I had been so happy. But it felt more than that. Later, I got chatting to a neighbour on the ground floor, a pensioner who knew everyone's business.

"I bumped into a young mum with a pram earlier," I said. "She had a right shiner, poor thing. Does she live in this block?"

The old lady nodded.

"I know the girl you mean," she said. "She's had a rough time. Her adopted mum runs a cafe, down the precinct."

As she spoke, I suddenly felt my legs buckle beneath me. I knew that Jasmine, my daughter, had been adopted into a family who owned a cafe. But surely it was just a coincidence, and nothing more. There were tens of thousands of adoptions and tens of thousands of cafes, I reminded myself.

"Calm down, Carol," I told myself silently.

But I was shaking as I made an excuse to rush back home. Once I was inside, I called Ava.

"You'll never believe this," I said. "There's a girl in this block who was adopted and her mum runs a cafe. Just like Jasmine!"

Ava sucked in her breath.

"I'm on my way round," she replied.

Within minutes, she was at my doorstep.

"Let's go down to the council office," she said. "See what we can find out."

Together, we went down to the offices, and I stood at the desk, trembling, and told them my story.

"I'm afraid I can't give out any information," said the housing officer.

"Please," I begged. "She's an adult now. I need to know if it's her. She has a right to know me, too."

I gave the officer Jasmine's name and date of birth but of course I knew her name would be different now.

"Can you just tell me if there is anyone living in my block of flats with this date of birth?" I asked.

She typed something into a computer and suddenly, her face blanched.

"I can't give you any information at all," she stuttered. "You would have to speak to social services. I really can't help, as I said."

But I knew. Deep down, I'd known since the moment I saw her on the stairs. The connection was visceral. I couldn't explain it. Ava and I walked back to my flat in shocked silence. The coincidence had struck us both dumb.

"Why don't you just knock on her door and explain everything?" Ava suggested.

I shook my head. There was no way I could do that, not to Jasmine or to myself. Besides, I was a dithering wreck. I could hardly speak, never mind about introduce myself to my long-lost daughter. Every single day since the adoption, I had thought of her. But never had I imagined that we would one day be reunited, living just a few feet away from each other. I had been living in my new flat for six months, and this was the first time I had ever seen her.

"Would you like me to knock on her door instead?" Ava offered. "I could find out if it's really Jasmine first of all, and then see how she feels about meeting you."

I nodded gratefully. We decided to leave it until the following day, for Ava to prepare herself. Early the next morning, she came round again.

"Wish me luck," she smiled.

I was shivering so hard that my teeth were chattering. I

followed Ava at a safe distance, so that I couldn't be seen. I heard her knock on the door and someone answered.

"I think you and me might be related," I heard Ava say. "What's your name, duck?"

"Jasmine," the girl replied.

It was all I could do not to cry out. I felt tears welling inside me, like a dam about to burst. She had kept the same name, after all. The name I had chosen for her.

"And are you adopted?" Ava pressed.

I was straining to listen, but I couldn't hear the response. And then, I heard the girl say:

"It was Mackie. Jasmine Mackie."

I allowed myself to sink to the floor, with my head in my hands. This felt like a crazy dream. I could hear Ava telling Jasmine that she was indeed her aunt, and that her natural mother was living just a few doors away.

"Would you like to meet her?" Ava asked. "At least have a think about it?"

Fearful of the response, I fled back indoors, with my hands clapped over my ears. Moments later, Ava appeared in the doorway.

"It's her!" she announced, her face shining with tears. "It's your little Jazzy."

"What did she say?" I whispered. "Will she meet me?"

Ava nodded.

"I think so," she said. "She's in shock, she's bound to be! But she said she'll come and see you, when she's ready."

The emotion was like a golf ball in my throat. All day I waited, but she didn't come. I didn't even like to nip to the loo in case I missed her knock. That night, I lay awake, with my mind whirring. The coincidence was mind-blowing. When Jasmine was adopted, she could have gone to live anywhere in the whole world. And yet here she was, living in the same block of flats as me.

There were three precious people in my life: Sunny, Jasmine and Karl. I had thought Sunny would be around forever, but he was gone. I had thought Jasmine would be lost forever, and now she was here. I couldn't make sense of it. I felt as though Sunny dying and Jasmine appearing were somehow connected. It felt as though fate had thrown us together – and just at the time when I needed her the most.

The next day, my doorbell went, and I froze. I opened it, as if in slow motion, and it seemed to take years before it swung wide – and there she was. My Jasmine. She was a young woman, and a mother herself now, to a new baby. That made me a grandmother!

"I've never stopped thinking of you," I said softly. "I never wanted you to be adopted."

I realised how lame that sounded, but it was all I could say. Jasmine had darker skin and hair and she was smaller and slimmer than me. But facially, we were identical. We stood side by side, in the mirror, and the resemblance was striking. She looked exactly like me as a young woman.

"Tell me everything," I urged. "I've missed so much."

I wanted everything to slot into place, but it was awkward and stilted between us. I yearned so much for us to be friends and to be close. But Jasmine had had her own troubles. She was wary, understandably. And I sensed she was angry, too.

"Let's take it slowly," I suggested.

That same week, I took Karl to see her. He had always known about his sister and I hoped they would get on well. But I could see, from that first meeting, that they had little in common. Karl was a teenage boy, she was a young mum. They had been raised differently.

Over the next few months, I strived to make up for what we had lost. I babysat as much as I could, and I cooked for Jasmine, too. I loved it most when we just sat and chatted, catching up on the past. I explained that my parents wouldn't allow me to keep a baby of colour, and that I had nowhere to live and nobody to rely on.

"I was given no choice," I told her again and again. "I was in a bad frame of mind."

I didn't tell her about Ian, or about Aston Hall. I didn't want to upset her more than I needed. At first, Jasmine seemed to accept what I was saying. I did most of the talking, and she was quiet and rather shy. We settled into a routine, with her coming round most days. Often, I'd babysit when she went out shopping. One day, she said to me:

"Do you want anything from the supermarket, Mum?"

Choking back the tears, I shook my head. I loved her calling me Mum.

The following year, Jasmine had another baby and moved into a bigger place, not far away. Then she got married and had more children. Her life seemed chaotic, and though we saw a lot of each other, our relationship was becoming strained. I didn't always like the way she was behaving. But then, I understood that it really was none of my business. She had every right to be critical of me, too. Even so, the arguments continued. Sadly, eventually, I had to concede that too much had happened and too much damage had been done. I could not whitewash over the traumas of the past, as I had hoped. We saw less and less of each other and, though it broke my heart, I had to admit that it was probably for the best.

"You did your best, Mum," Karl said to me.

But it felt like it wasn't enough. It was not lost on me that I struggled to form lasting relationships. I had lost touch with so many people who should, ordinarily, have been close to me. Sometimes, it seemed the harder I tried, the more likely I was to fail. At times, as with my parents, it just felt impossible. I had seen my mother, occasionally, over the years, always by chance. But there was no thaw between us. I heard, through Ava, that she had been diagnosed with bowel cancer, but I felt it best to stay away. One night, in July 2004, I was woken by Karl shaking me by the shoulder.

"Mum, wake up, Aunty Ava's on the phone," he said. "Your mum's in hospital. It's serious."

I rubbed my eyes and took the phone from him.

"I thought you might want to visit," Ava said. "Mum's dying. It's your call."

For hours, I agonised over whether to visit. Why should I, after the way she had treated me? By dawn, as the first streaks of light poked through my curtains, I had made my decision. I got dressed and walked to the bus stop. When I found the ward, Mum looked pale and weak. I sat at her bedside and moved my chair in close. She turned to me, her head on the pillow, and said:

"Why haven't you visited me, all these years?"

I sighed. Even now, on her deathbed, she had nothing but recriminations for me. Nothing had changed.

"Think about how you treated me, all these years," I replied. "That's why."

I walked out of the hospital, knowing it had been a mistake to even think that we might be reconciled. I had given her chance after chance and made it easy for her, over the years, to make up for her mistakes or put them behind us. But she obviously either didn't want forgiveness or didn't feel she needed it.

She died that same week, aged 74. I didn't attend her funeral, and afterwards, I didn't visit her grave. I wanted no reminders of the ways in which she had failed me and my son. As a frightened child, I had gone to her for help, confiding in her about the abuse I was suffering, and she hadn't even had the decency to hear me out. She had dismissed me with a flap of her hand, as though I was an annoying fly. All through my teenage years, she'd made no effort to bring me home from Aston Hall or Craigmore Hostel. I hated to think about it, but I'm sure she liked me being away. And when Karl was born, she refused even to look at his beautiful face. She was the worst kind of mother and grandmother, and now that she was dead I felt only sadness for the suffering she had caused.

In the years that followed, I concentrated on working hard. Karl settled down close by with a partner, and they went on to have three daughters. I adored them and made sure, above all, that I had time to listen to them. I still suffered with nervous tics, panic attacks and anxiety – and my temper was always there, bubbling away, under the surface. At night, I had to have two mattresses, to make sure I was high up – too high to be pinned down. Yet even then, I was still plagued by nightmares, where Ian would hold me down and squash my chest with such force that I woke, gasping for breath, with my heart pounding against my ribs. I saw my doctor and explained I was struggling with anxiety, but I was prescribed more pills.

"I've had enough pills to last me a lifetime," I replied. "They won't help me."

I was referred for counselling instead, but that wasn't for me either. Much as I tried, I just couldn't bring myself to talk about the abuse. I preferred to bury it instead.

One day, in 2010, I was out shopping in Derby city centre, and I decided to pop into Wilkos. I fancied treating myself to a new dinner service, and I hoped I might find a bargain in there. I had only just gone through the doors when I felt someone staring at me, from behind. It was so powerful, it was almost magnetic. A shiver ran right through me, like an electric jolt. Nervously, I turned around, and came face to face with Ian. At once, the breath drained from me. I felt so weak, I almost sank to the floor in the middle of the shop. He was so close, I could see the saliva on his yellowy teeth. I closed my eyes and for a moment I was once again lying on the bed, pinned to the mattress, unable to breathe.

"Oh, look who's here," he gloated. "Why aren't you talking? Cat got your tongue?"

There it was again. The control. I was a grown woman, yet he still thought he could bully me. I was the Daddy Long Legs, and he was pulling my legs off, one by one, and laughing as I suffered and shrivelled in front of him.

"Well?" Ian demanded. "Aren't you going to say hello to your big brother?"

Inside, I was screaming. He was no brother of mine. But I said nothing. I ran outside, without my shopping, and jumped straight into a taxi home. I held my head in my hands for the entire journey home. But by the time we pulled up outside my flat, I felt not scared, but furious. How dare he confront me like that?

"It's time to get a hold of yourself," I said firmly. "You're not a kid anymore. This has gone on long enough."

My bravado only lasted until night time. For as I was getting undressed for bed, I felt sick with anxiety. My bed was already high enough for me to see out of the window. But that night, I slept with the curtains open, too. I had to have a way of escaping, through windows without bars, from a bed without a captor. As I drifted off to sleep, I felt that same pressure on my chest, I felt a sharp pain down below, I felt the breath being squeezed from my lungs. I woke up, shivering and sweating all at once.

"I can't go on like this," I muttered.

I knew I had to confide in Karl. I had never told him the truth about my childhood, hoping to spare him the agonies I knew it would bring. He knew of course that I was at odds with my family, but we had never discussed it too deeply. He knew I had had anxiety and anger issues, but again, he thought nothing of it. I realised now that it was best to be honest.

"Karl, I need to tell you something," I said sadly. "And you're not going to like it."

"Is this about your childhood?" he asked.

I nodded. He had suspected something was wrong, after all. He had been waiting for my revelation. But his face crumpled as all the jigsaw pieces of my fragmented childhood tumbled out, one by one. It was so hard, seeing his face twist in disbelief and anger.

"I can't believe they put you through that," he kept saying. "You should have told me, Mum."

"I didn't want to upset you," I explained. "I'm sorry."

"To be honest, it makes a lot of sense," he said. "I understand now why you are the way you are."

I shrugged sadly. I had tried to blot it all out. But clearly I hadn't been as successful as I'd hoped.

"I'm telling you now because I don't know what to do," I told him. "I feel like maybe I'd feel better if it was out in the open."

He put his hand over mine.

"It's up to you," he replied. "I don't want to force you to go to the police, it has to be your decision. But I'll support you all the way. It's time your voice was heard."

Afterwards, I felt relieved. I hadn't expected this, but I felt so much better, just for sharing my secret with my son. It meant so much, to have his support. I was scared though. Keeping secrets was hard. But speaking out might be even harder. It was a risk I had to take. I remembered Sunny's last words to me:

"Don't let people walk all over you…"

"I won't," I said softly. "I promise, love."

It was his final wish that I spoke out and got justice, and I owed it to him, to Karl, to myself – and to everyone who had ever lived with abuse and fear. With quivering hands, I called the police. I wasn't sure they'd even take me seriously. It was so long ago and there was no physical evidence. I had scrubbed it all away.

Chapter Nineteen

"I want to report a crime," I said nervously.

I was given a time, later that week, to attend the station. It was a sunny morning, in August 2010, when my appointment came around. I woke early, my whole body tense and wired. I wasn't sure I could go through with this. I arrived at the police station, but when I reached the doors, I froze. I just couldn't go inside.

For 20 minutes, I paced up and down the pavement, trying to pluck up the courage to walk through the doors. Eventually, swallowing down my panic and my doubts, I marched inside.

"Carol Minto," I told the desk sergeant. "I'm here to make my complaint."

Inside the interview room, I was joined by a male officer. My heart sank. There was no way I could speak to a man, I just couldn't do it. I didn't think he'd want to hear it either. With my nerves jangling, I stood in the corner of the room, like a frightened animal.

"Take a seat," said the officer, showing me a chair.

"I don't want to," I said. "I've changed my mind. I don't think it's a good idea."

The officer looked at me kindly.

"I want to listen to you," he said. "And I've got all day. Honestly, as long as it takes."

His words put me at ease. I edged towards the chair, but my whole body was shaking. Now that I was so close, those last few inches seemed like miles. I felt as though I was staring over the edge of a cliff, and it was so far down, I felt dizzy.

"Let's start with the reason you're here," said the officer gently. "As I said, there's no rush."

Somehow, I blurted it out.

"I have to call him my brother, so you can make sense of it," I said. "But I no longer see him as a brother. He's a monster."

The officer brought in a colleague, a lady this time, and together they sat and listened to the story of my childhood. With each detail, I relived it. It was so hard. But I gritted my teeth, screwed my eyes shut, and got on with it. I was doing this for Karl, as well as myself. I wanted to show him – and my grandchildren, and all other victims of abuse – that suffering in silence was not the best way. At the end, the officer shook my hand.

"Thank you, Carol," he said. "Thank you for coming forward."

Arrangements were made for me to make a second

statement the following week, at a specialist unit for sexual abuse cases. This time, it was a homely looking bungalow, with sofas and a coffee table. I was told I was being filmed and watched by specially trained officers. But the comfy chairs did nothing to ease my dread and going through it again was no easier this time around. There were moments when I was so crippled with shame and fear that I felt paralysed. I opened and closed my mouth, but the words just didn't come.

"Take your time, Carol," said the officer gently.

But all the way through, from that first moment, I felt as though I was being taken seriously. I felt as though these people cared. Eventually, I reached the point in my story where I had been taken to Aston Hall by the social workers.

"And then it started again," I said. "More abuse, more suffering. Only this time, it was Dr Milner. He made my life a misery."

The officer's eyes widened.

"This ought to form part of a different complaint," she said. "It's something you must pursue, after the case against your brother is finished."

I nodded. Though at that moment, I really didn't feel as though I had the strength. After my interview, the police told me that Ian would be questioned. I was on tenterhooks, waiting to see what the outcome would be. It was 46 years, after all, since the abuse. Perhaps I had left it too long? I tried not to think about it in the days that followed, knowing that I was likely to be facing bad news. But then the police called.

"Your brother has been charged," the officer announced. "The case is going ahead. This is the oldest historical sexual abuse case we've ever dealt with."

I put the phone down, and within my chest, I felt a rising sense of optimism and hope. Maybe, just maybe, justice was in sight. Word got around that Ian had been charged, and it wasn't long before various members of my family called and confronted me.

"Why are you saying this?" they demanded. "Why are you telling lies? Why rake up the past?"

I slammed the phone down in anger. Nobody offered me any support. Nobody considered that I might actually be telling the truth. But I was used to that by now and though it was upsetting, I didn't let it get me down. One day, I bumped into my dad whilst I was out shopping.

"I wish you'd just leave this business alone," he said to me. "You're dragging your own brother through the courts. And for what? What will people think of our family?"

"Is that all you're bothered about?" I replied furiously. "Don't I matter more than what people think? What about the truth? Isn't that important?"

"I'm just thinking of the family name, that's all," Dad replied.

"I have no family," I replied sadly. "I've never had a

family. I've always been on my own. And as for the court case, I won't leave it alone. I won't be silenced any longer."

One year on, in October 2011, Ian Mackie appeared at Derby Crown Court charged with indecent assault and gross indecency, against more than one victim. He pleaded not guilty to the offences and so I had to attend the hearing. I was frightened, but I was also determined. I had come this far, and now, all I wanted was for the world to know the truth. Karl and his partner took time off work to support me and Karl looked after their children at home so that his partner could be with me in the court. I had a liaison officer, too, and together we sat in a small room, in the court building, waiting for my name to be called. Every nerve in my body jangled and the minutes seemed to drag. Eventually, early in the afternoon, the officer said:

"Let me go and see what's happening. I won't be long."

When she returned, she was smiling broadly.

"I think he's going to plead guilty," she announced. "It's over, Carol. You did it."

I had expected to feel euphoric. But her words, if anything, were something of an anti-climax. After all, I had always known that he was guilty. This was not a revelation for me. Ian pleaded guilty to indecently assaulting me between 1965 and 1967 and the prosecutor said it was the oldest sexual abuse case he had come across. He had also been charged with other offences and some charges were left to lie on file.

Ian was sentenced that same afternoon to five years' imprisonment and was ordered to sign the sex offenders' register for life. I did not go into court to hear his fate, but I felt it was a fair result. Ian deserved to be punished. More than that, people deserved to know what sort of beast he really was. The police officer told me that the judge had specifically mentioned Aston Hall in his final speech.

"The judge said that he was unable to deal with the issues at Aston Hall in this court, but that he urges you to continue with a complaint," she told me. "See, people are on your side. You must carry on, Carol."

The announcement blindsided me, almost more than the sentencing. This was the first time the horrors of Aston Hall had been referred to publicly. Of course I'd talked about Dr Milner in my police interviews, and it was all formally recorded. But it still felt hidden and private, somehow. This was different. Having it said out loud – in a court of law – gave me hope. It felt like a big moment, like I was finally getting somewhere.

I was pleased that justice was done. But there was no celebration. More than anything, I felt relieved and exhausted now that it was all over.

"It's not over yet," my support officer reminded me again, as we said goodbye on the court steps. "Remember Aston Hall. Remember to make a formal complaint, as soon as you feel ready."

I nodded.

"I won't let it go," I promised her. "Can you do me one final favour, and let my family know about the results of the trial? I can't face them."

With the exception of Ava, nobody had a kind word to say to me. I owed them nothing. But I wanted them to know, nevertheless, that I had been telling the truth. All those years, I had carried it around with me.

"Of course, the officer agreed. "I'll make sure they all know."

As soon as I got home, that very same afternoon, I rang the police again. This time, I had no misgivings. I was confident and self-assured. I had done it once. I could do it again.

"I want to make a complaint about Dr Kenneth Milner," I told them. "I was physically and sexually abused at Aston Hall in the late 1960s."

"We'll have to arrange for you to be interviewed by specialist officers," I was told.

"That's fine," I replied. "I can wait."

I decided to apply for copies of my medical records, too. I had so many unanswered questions about my teenage years and I needed to know what had happened to me, however painful that might be. Derby Social Services told me that my records had been destroyed, because it was so long ago.

"We're so sorry, we can't help," they told me.

I had not expected them to co-operate. After all, they

never had in the past. So next, I contacted the NHS Trust, with the help of a solicitor.

"We do have your records, but you will need to see a psychiatrist before they can be released to you," I was told.

"Yes, that's no problem," I said.

At the appointment, the psychiatrist looked down his glasses at me and said:

"Are you absolutely sure you want these records? They make very difficult reading, you know. I must warn you."

"Difficult reading!" I snapped. "This actually happened to me. It was difficult to survive, never mind read about, I can tell you that. Of course, I'm sure I want them. I'm not 15 years of age, not any more."

That night, I settled onto the couch with a cup of tea and I opened my file. It was so thick, I hadn't expected so much paperwork. As I read, I felt myself leapfrogging back to my teenage years, back to Aston Hall. I found a note I had written to Dr Milner, after spending the weekend at home. I had completely forgotten about it until it fell out of my file onto the carpet, but suddenly, it all came flooding back. I had written because I wanted to see him to ask if I could go home for another visit. But he never answered my letter. Then, I found a report from Dr Milner, which claimed that I was "prone to fantasy". I almost choked on the irony. Of course, that strategy worked perfectly for him. He had simply dismissed all his patients as fantasists, liars and delinquents, so that if and when they complained about him, they would never be taken seriously and he would never be held to account. He was plotting his own defence, covering his own back, all the way through. He had made sure that we would never be heard.

Or so he thought.

"You slimy old worm," I said to myself.

There were copies of drug charts, too. Daily records of the way I had been sedated, silenced and abused.

"Barbitone sodium, 300mg, chlorpromazine, 25mg," I read. "No wonder I was so zonked out."

I even found a copy of the result of the gonorrhoea test, which was negative. I had waited 40 years for the result!

I came across letters relating to sickness benefits, which had apparently been paid out on my behalf during my time at Aston Hall and Craigmore Hostel, ceasing when I began work at the factory. I hadn't ever known about the payments and I certainly hadn't been given any money.

To my surprise, there was a letter from my Scottish grandmother. Tears spilled down my face as I read:

'I am the grandmother of Carol Mackie... I would like to know more of her illness as neither Carol or her parents gave me any satisfactory explanation...'

I could hear her soft voice and her lilting Scottish vowels as I read and reread her words. It was so cathartic for me. All those years I had thought nobody missed me, nobody cared. But I had been wrong. She had tried to find out what had become of me.

"Thank you," I whispered, my chest bursting with emotion. "Thank you, Granny, for loving me."

But just as the warmth was flooding through me, the contents of the next page snapped my heart in two. I found a letter, sent to my parents from Sister Clackton, a week after my admission to Aston Hall, telling them exactly where I was.

"Your daughter has been admitted to Laburnum Ward, Aston Hall."

I read it again, sure there had been some mistake. But then I spotted another letter, this time from social services, confirming the same information.

"They knew!" I gasped. "They knew!"

All along, they had known just where to find me. Yet apart from that one occasion, when Dad had arrived in his van, they had never bothered to call or write or come to see me. Worse still, they had lied to me, pretending they had no idea where I was being held. I recalled a conversation with Dad where he insisted he had driven around the city, searching for me. That simply was not true. They both knew I was at Aston Hall. But they did not want to see me. They did not even write to me. One record stated that my mother had actually asked for my visit home to be cancelled, because the other children had chicken pox. I didn't believe that for a moment. She just wanted to put off having me home. Another letter, from social services, said:

"For most of her stay here (at Aston Hall), (Carol)

has been in conflict about her home which she appears to be rejecting, the family showing no positive interest in her. Her last two weekends at home appear to have been disastrous…"

I was almost 50 years old, but still the words slashed through me. My family had showed no positive interest in me. Reading it in black and white seemed to make the truth more concrete, more unavoidable, somehow. And infinitely more harrowing. Angrily, I screwed the letter up inside my balled fist and clutched my head in my hands, sobbing and wailing.

All my life, I had asked myself what I had done to deserve such cruelty. How had I been at fault? What could I have done to avoid this? Now, reading through reams and reams of evidence which pointed the finger directly at Ian, at Milner, at my parents, I had the answer. I had done nothing wrong. *This had all been done to me.* The shift was seismic and it left me limp with exhaustion.

The following day, I showed Karl the records, but he was unable to stomach reading them.

"If someone took my child away, I wouldn't give up on them," he told me fiercely. "I would wait on the doorstep, outside social services, until I had answers. I would never give up. Never."

His anger towards my family burned brighter than ever that day, and I felt an immense pride in him.

"I know you would," I said. "And you are absolutely

right, Karl. You've grown up to be a good man and a great father."

I could comfort myself that at least I had got one thing right in life. Sunny and I had raised a wonderful son.

*****

Three weeks on from my call to the police, I got a call from a chief inspector and we made arrangements for two officers to visit me at home.

First of all, I had to give a physical description of Dr Milner and of Aston Hall. Then, I moved on to talking about the injections, the treatment room and the daily drug routines.

"I was forced to wear a strait jacket," I told them, shuddering. "I was tied up and made to answer the same questions, over and over again.

"And yet Milner never listened to anything I said. I told him I was being abused at home. I asked him to help me. Instead, he just ignored me and then he abused me himself."

It wasn't easy, going over the past, but in some ways the court case against Ian had been good preparation. I had learned to steel myself when dredging up the worst of my memories, and simply spit them out. There was no other way.

I even found I could talk to male, as well as female

officers. For me, and for the investigation, it was a step forward.

"You've been a great help, Carol," said the officers. "This is horrific stuff."

It turned out I was the very first person in Derby to make a complaint about Aston Hall. As a result, an investigation on behalf of all the children there was opened. Little did I know it, but I was opening the biggest can of worms. This was the beginning of the end of years of trauma for so many women – and I was proud to be the first one to speak out. This for me was more helpful to my recovery than any medication or counselling sessions could ever have been.

My life had a new feeling of stability and calm.

But as is often the case, my good news was quickly followed by tragedy, and I got a call from Ava which made my heart sink.

"My cancer's back."

Chapter Twenty

Ava had had breast cancer some years earlier and had been given the all-clear. But now, it was back again. Over the next few months, she grew weaker and she had to use a wheelchair. I took her out for walks around the local park or for a spot of shopping. I hoped against hope that she might beat it a second time. But it wasn't to be. Ava died in June 2012, and I felt absolutely wretched. Of my entire family, she and I had always been the closest.

I attended her funeral, but after the church service, I slipped away before the wake. I couldn't face anyone in my family. Even now that Ian had been convicted – especially now that Ian had been convicted – I felt like an outsider.

Throughout the remainder of 2012, I was interviewed five or six times by officers from Operation Hydrant, a team dealing with allegations of historical child sex abuse. The detectives visited me at home each time, gathering more and more evidence. I was told that, as a result of my complaint, they were also interviewing other patients, other victims. The operation became so big that it became a separate inquiry and was renamed Operation Thalia.

"It's important that you don't make contact with any other victims," the police told me. "It could jeopardise the case."

I understood completely. It was hard though, keeping it all to myself. Talking about Aston Hall brought back vivid flashbacks. I could smell the bleach again. I could hear the hot water pipes grumbling and complaining. I remembered the crush each morning as we jostled for clean laundry. I could feel my heart dropping with a thud, as the gauze was dropped over my face and everything around me went black.

More than anything, I recalled the boredom. The sheer inactivity, day after day, of being drugged and dumped in the hall, like an experiment discarded part way through and abandoned.

The nightmares returned too – with a vengeance. Sometimes, I woke up shouting, arms flailing, convinced that there were blocks on my windows and that I was locked in. I fancied, through the darkness, that I could hear the clip clip of Nurse Clackton's shoes along the wooden floor.

But despite this increased trauma, there was an overriding sense of relief and comfort. For so long, I had been mute, sedated and silenced, either through medication or through my own fear. And now, all that was about to change. At last, at last, our voices were being heard. I remembered old Doris, with her faithful dog. I remembered the poor girls locked in Rowan Ward, smearing their own faeces up the walls, their faces yellow through lack of sunlight. I thought of Tania, running away and scratching herself on the brambles and of Sandy, dear sweet Sandy, who treated me like a sister. I wept when I saw their faces in my dreams.

This was about doing the right thing. For everyone.

The police came to see me again, but this time I learned that Dr Milner had died in 1975.

"He would have faced questioning if he was alive," they told me. "But of course, there will be no charges against him now. We're so sorry, Carol. That doesn't mean of course that the investigation stops here."

I had suspected Dr Milner might be dead. He had seemed to be an old man even when I was at Aston Hall, but of course that was from the perspective of a young girl. I had no idea how old he really was. Even so, the news left me feeling deflated. I needed to face him, I desperately wanted to tell him how many lives he had destroyed. I would have loved for him to suffer just a tiny taste of the humiliation and despair that we had lived with, every day, at Aston Hall. Now, that would never happen.

Midway through 2013, a witness care officer contacted me to say that Ian was about to be released from prison. I already knew that his sentence had been reduced on appeal, to two and a half years. The news had been on the radio some months earlier, even before I'd received the letter from the police. It angered me that he was wriggling away from his punishment, even now.

I thought back to when he was little, blaming me for everything that went wrong. He had pushed me in the pond and blamed me. He had punched my playmates and shifted the guilt onto me. Now he was an adult and still he couldn't accept responsibility for his wrongdoings. And incredibly, he was about to walk free.

"He will not be allowed to contact you, directly or indirectly," the officer assured me.

The announcement did not floor me as I might have expected. After all, I had known this day was coming. And I was done with Ian. He had ruined too much of my life already and now, I vowed to myself, I would not give him any more time or thought. Even so, I couldn't escape hearing the gossip from my family.

"Ian is living in a bungalow," Dad told me, when I bumped into him at the shops one day. "He's doing OK."

"I don't want to hear it," I snapped.

My dad was becoming an old man, and I didn't want to argue with him any longer. But it stung that he never apologised for what had happened to me. He didn't seem to think he had done anything wrong. And though he condemned Ian, he refused to disown him.

"He's my son," he said pathetically. "What can I do?"

I hoped if my son had ever done anything so reprehensible, that I would have the strength to stand up for my beliefs. But old habits die hard and I said nothing to Dad.

In 2016, again whilst I was out shopping, Dad informed me that Ian had died. For a moment, I felt a shiver run through me. But then I forced myself to refocus.

"Why are you telling me this?" I asked. "I'm not interested. I don't want to know what he died from. I don't want any more details."

To me, he had been dead for many years anyway.

A few months later, Dad became ill himself. Up until then, I had held back from visiting him at home. We were not that close these days. But I heard that he had back pain and was passing blood and I knew he needed my help. Swallowing the bitterness of the past, I knocked on his door.

"I've come to see if you need anything," I said. "I could pop to the supermarket for you. And how about I give this place a clean?"

Dad smiled gratefully.

"You're a good daughter," he told me.

Over the next few weeks, I began looking after him regularly. I was with at the hospital, too, when he was diagnosed with cancer. But despite his age, he was determined to fight it.

"I'm not going anywhere until I'm ready," he told me firmly.

As he grew weaker, I visited more often, cooking and cleaning and keeping him company. It was like the old days, in many ways. Nostalgically, I remembered our trip to France with the racing pigeons, I thought of him arriving at Aston Hall with my dog Peter yapping away on the passenger seat. But just as quickly, I remembered the letter from Sister Clackton, informing my parents where I was. He had done nothing about that for a whole year. And that fateful phrase "the family showing no positive interest in her" was burned across my brain. I could try to forgive. But I could never forget. One day, as I was washing the dishes, Dad said to me:

"I don't want to be a burden to you, Carol, I don't like you doing all this housework for me."

It was on the tip of my tongue to say: "You didn't mind me doing it all as a child, did you?"

But I gulped back the words. It would do no good to pick an argument with him now. He was taken into hospital, and we knew the end was near, but even then, he didn't mention Mum. Not once. I was unsure whether he was sparing my feelings, or his own. He died in August 2017, aged 86, and I adopted his little Jack Russell, Diddy, who is still with me to this day. She has a Scottish flag on her collar, a nod to happier times and to my beloved Scottish family.

I didn't go to Dad's funeral because I couldn't bear the pitying stares and cruel whispers from relatives. But I often visited his grave afterwards. At weekends, I'd take flowers to the cemetery for Dad, Ava and of course, my beloved Sunny.

Through the inquiry into Aston Hall, I hooked up again with the other women who had been locked up there. In my mind, they were all still girls, just as I had left them. It was something of a surprise to find out they were mothers and grandmothers, just like me. There was even a survivors' Facebook group, but we had to be careful not to discuss the abuse in detail. Really, the only two people I wanted to see were Sandy and Tania.

I had been in touch with both of my pals, on and off, over the years, but it had been several years since I'd seen either of them.

Firstly, I went to Tania's address, a neat two-bed terraced home, not far from me in Derby. But when the door opened, it was answered by a stranger, who informed me Tania had moved years earlier.

"Any idea where she went?" I asked.

The new owner shook his head, apologetically. Back at home, I began trawling Facebook and eventually I managed to track Tania down. By now, she was married and had a different surname, so it wasn't easy to find her. I had no sooner sent her a message than my inbox pinged with a reply.

"Call me!" Tania wrote, including her number. "Now!"

It was great just to hear her voice. We arranged to meet up the following day, at the bus station cafe. The cosy cafe had been a port in a storm for me throughout my life, and once again, it was about to witness a momentous moment.

I'd hidden at the bus station as a runaway teen. I'd worked at the cafe, as a desperate twenty-something. And now, I was about to meet my dear friend there once again. I hadn't seen Tania since Karl was a child.

"Wow, you haven't changed one bit!" she beamed, giving me a big hug.

But Tania had certainly changed. She had mellowed so much since our crazy days at Aston Hall. Once our ringleader, always full of beans and ideas, now she was calm and thoughtful.

"It's all down to my new husband," she told me with a smile. "I feel really settled with him."

When she told me his name, my jaw dropped. He and I had been at the same school together!

"Do you know about the inquiry?" I asked Tania. "The police are looking for statements. They want witness accounts."

Tania shrugged.

"I really can't remember much," she admitted. "I don't know whether my mind is fuddled by all those drugs they pumped into us. Or maybe my subconscious has blocked it all out. But I really can't remember much at all, Carol."

In some ways, I envied her. I was tormented by my memories. Yet I knew it was important to remember, important to expose what we had been through. Vital to ensure it never happened again. Tania and I arranged to meet up again the following week.

"I'll never lose touch with you again," I vowed.

And I kept my word. We became firm friends, best friends, and remain so to this day.

After finding Tania, I set about contacting Sandy, too. I knew where to find her, she worked in a shopping centre in Derby, but as with Tania, our contact had slipped over the years. That same week, I went into the centre and she spotted me from far away.

"Ah, my bestest friend!" Sandy called, her eyes shiny with tears.

We arranged to meet up after work, at the bus station cafe. Strangely, as I waited, I felt tears pricking my eyes. Sandy and I had seen each other a few times since our teenage years, but always, it was about burying the past. We never talked about it. But now, we were meeting up to face the past head on, all guns blazing. It was such a powerful emotion. Sandy had been in Aston Hall longer than I had and she remembered it vividly.

"We've done well to come through it all," she told me. "No child should suffer like we did."

"And hopefully no child ever will again," I replied quietly.

In 2018, the report into Aston Hall was finally published. The police called in advance to warn me it was out.

"It makes for grim reading," they said.

"Oh, I know that," I replied. "I was there."

But even for me, the findings were stomach-churning.

The sheer scale of the abuse and the suffering was mind-boggling. Twelve police officers had collated 114 witness statements, recorded 73 crimes – including 33 instances of physical abuse and 40 sexual – and heard 140 witness accounts. The dates of the allegations ranged from 1954 to 1979.

It revealed that Aston Hall had been used as a Red Cross Hospital during the First World War. In 1925, it was developed into a colony for people with learning disabilities and became a treatment centre for children with learning impairments and mental health issues. Children in care from across the country were placed there by local authorities, both for long term treatment and weekend care.

Dr Milner was recorded as holding the title of Physician Superintendent of Aston Hall. I remembered him announcing his title to me on my first day there. I had actually thought, naively, that he might be the one to help me.

The report continued:

Treatment methods at Aston Hall Hospital are known to have included sedation; where young people were put to sleep to allow memory testing, often referred to as 'Narco-analysis'. This involved interviewing patients in a drug induced state in order that they recall and disclose thoughts and feelings that they would normally conceal.

In Narco-analysis, patients were injected with sodium pentothal or sodium amytal.

It was terrifying seeing it written down. But I felt

strangely euphoric, too. At last, people were taking notice. At last, our voices were being heard.

And it went on:

This type of procedure would not be acceptable within today's medical standards. It is questionable as to whether it was acceptable during the period in question, particularly in the treatment of young people... Many patients were sent to Aston Hall without prior contact from clinical staff. There are a number of patients who have suggested that they were hand-picked to attend Aston Hall. Complainants were under the age of 18 at the time they allege to have been victims of abuse at Aston Hall.

The report went on to describe what happened in the treatment room, step by step. The lonely mattress on the floor, the strait jacket, the slow drip of the ether. It was chillingly accurate. Afterwards, the report stated that Milner had not documented or recorded the treatment in any way. That was no surprise to me. I had always known we were there for his gratification and nothing more. He wasn't at all interested in research or in what we had to say.

The report included advice from a specialist called Professor Simon Wessely. He provided an opinion based upon the information he received: that there were no consent issues in the 1960s, a doctor would do what he / she felt necessary, that patients are more likely to talk of sexual matters when under sodium amytal but it is highly suggestible. Patients could make things up. He could not understand the use of ether with sodium amytal and could not explain why a strait jacket would be used. He spoke about Largactil, a major tranquilliser, being used a lot on children in the 60s.

The report concluded that, had he been alive, Milner would most certainly have been questioned in relation to sexual and physical offences against the children in his care.

It was draining reading through the facts. It seemed so far-fetched, so ghoulish and wicked, yet I knew that every word was true.

In the days afterwards, I was left feeling rather hollow. Perhaps I had expected, with the publication of such a damning report, that the world would judder to a halt. That people would be outraged and apoplectic at the way we had been treated. But that was not the way. There were media reports of course, and I gave interviews along with some of the other women. But slowly, life returned to normal, and I conceded that was probably for the best.

I had refused to let Ian invade my thoughts and now it was vital not to let the report dominate my consciousness, too. The whole point of making my complaints was so that I could put this behind me and move on. And I tried to focus on that.

In 2019, I was awarded compensation for my ordeal: £14,000 for my suffering at Aston Hall and £8000 for the abuse from Ian. It beggared belief. My solicitor worked out I had endured 20 separate treatments at Dr Milner's hands, comprising of what – I dare not think. Certainly it's

Chapter Twenty

accepted as part of the official report, that I was sexually
abused and raped by Milner. I was also drugged and held
against my will. The payout was pitiful. I didn't want money,
but I wanted recognition of what I had been through. And
this felt like a slap in the face. Yet again, though, I refused
to allow myself to feel maudlin. I was determined to put
the money to good use and so to cheer myself up, I went
out shopping.

*****

Stepping out of the changing rooms, I wrapped the red
woollen coat around me and looked in the mirror.

"It looks lovely," smiled the sales assistant. "Just your
colour, too. It really suits you."

But as I fastened the belt one notch more, I felt a sharp
tightening around my waist. My arms and my legs felt
as though they were being crushed. It was as though an
invisible force was pushing and squeezing my limbs and
there was an icy pressure on my throat. Gasping, choking,
I tried to focus on the coat and the mirror and the warm
glow of the changing rooms, but it was all nothing more
than a red blur.

"Is everything alright?" asked the sales assistant. "You
look a bit pale."

She offered me a chair, and uncertainly I staggered
backwards to sit down. Flashing images scattered around

me, like falling embers of a firestorm. The needle plunging into my arm, the strait jacket pulling tightly across my chest, the gag stuffed in my mouth.

"I'll have her – Mackie, the little fair one. Bring her to the treatment room."

I shook my head vigorously, trying to banish the memories, knock them out of my head, once and for all.

"I'm fine, thank you," I said to the assistant with a fixed smile. "I think I just got a bit hot, that's all."

She nodded.

"Well, the coat looks fabulous. I'd treat yourself if I was you. Is it for a special occasion?"

I opened my mouth to reply but again, his face loomed large in my eyeline, his grey hair, plastered flat and greasy against his head and glistening with too much Brylcreem, his long, pointy nose with a forest of dark hairs up each nostril.

"Your nose is like Concorde," I'd told him cheekily, the thought sneaking out through my lips, like a bubble, before I had chance to snatch it back.

"You're very rude, Mackie," he'd replied, as he dropped the mask lightly over my face. "And you have a good imagination, too. But you really shouldn't tell such lies."

His voice, low and measured, was dripping with scorn and superiority.

"Such lies…"

The truth was out now, of course. It had taken nearly

50 years, but it was out now. And I wasn't the one lying. I wasn't the abuser. I wasn't the monster. And so yes, I suppose this was a special occasion, in a way.

The compensation money meant nothing for the horrors I'd endured. And worse still were the horrors I knew nothing about. But I'd hoped to put it to good use, buying myself a good winter coat, the sort of clothing I usually couldn't afford. But now, as I unbuckled the belt and slipped the coat back on the hanger, all I could see was the treatment room. The bare mattress, the syringe on the metal tray, the surgical gloves.

And his eyes, his cold, glassy eyes, leering down at me.

"Poor Mackie, poor little girl, the doctor will make you better now."

Epilogue

It was a sunny day early in 2020 when I decided to return to Aston Hall.

Partly, I wanted to banish the ghouls of the past; to stand there and look them in the eye without flinching. And I was curious too. Just plain nosy at what had become of the place which had for so long been both my home and my torture chamber.

It has been knocked down and redeveloped now, and there's a shiny new housing estate in place of the crumbling wards, the locked windows and the blank faces which stared from inside.

There is one building remaining however, the oldest and the most forbidding.

And as I stood on the driveway, a lady walked past and said:

"I used to work there, you know, years ago. I was a nurse at the old Aston Hall psychiatric hospital."

My eyes widened.

"I was a patient, as it happens," I shuddered.

"There was a lot went on in that place that shouldn't have," she said. "I hope you're OK."

I smiled and nodded.

"I'm doing really well," I replied.

Even so, as I stared at the old building, I knew I could never be tempted inside, not for anything. The fear of hearing the door click behind me, and of knowing there was no escape, would haunt me always. I was fine coming back, but only as long as I was out here in the fresh air.

In November 2020, I got a letter from the Health Secretary, Matt Hancock, and in it he apologised for our anguish. He wrote:

"I would like to assure you that I am deeply sorry for the care and treatment that you received at Aston Hall Hospital. I know that it is still very distressing for you to recall your experiences and that the passage of time has not diminished that.

"I want to assure you that what happened at Aston Hall has been taken very seriously and the NHS has worked closely with all the relevant agencies, including Derbyshire Constabulary, to identify the individuals involved in the treatment at Aston Hall.

"I can assure you that Dr Milner's death has not prevented a thorough and robust investigation of what happened."

I threw the letter down in annoyance. I wasn't ready to accept the apology or believe his assurances. In my mind, the pathetic levels of compensation paid out to the victims of Aston Hall were the clearest indicator of what the government really thought of us.

Now, as my story comes to a close, my overwhelming feeling is one of defiance.

I'm 67 years old and I have survived, against the odds, no matter what. I'm like a little rubber ball – you can throw me and bounce me as hard as you like – but I will never break. I'm so glad I made my complaints against Ian and against Dr Milner. Justice is a great healer, and I would urge anyone who is trapped in an abusive nightmare to speak out and shout it from the rooftops. Honestly, you will feel so much better.

I have friends with severe memory loss, friends with anxiety and depression, some who struggle to leave the house and all because of what they went through at Aston Hall. I still have a fear of crowds and closed spaces and I don't like concerts or big events. I have to be high up, especially in bed at night, and I always need to have an escape route – a window or a staircase, some way of reaching the fresh air.

Two years ago, I woke up having lost my sight overnight and without any warning. I was diagnosed with Bell's palsy and I am now blind in one eye and have some left-sided paralysis. But it doesn't hold me back.

I will always have some residual mental health issues, too, I've made my peace with that now. But I make damn sure that I have them – and they don't have me. I'm the one in charge these days. I like to think I'm a force to be reckoned with.

My friendships with my pals from Aston Hall have endured and grown stronger. Our bond is like no other. We are glued together by our shared history of trauma, but it's also peppered with fun and humour. I have a love of sewing, knitting and crocheting and I enjoy making gifts for my granddaughters. I must, I suppose, thank the Aston Hall sewing teacher for that, though it's through gritted teeth! I try to see the positives – and more than that, I try to see the funny side. I think that's why I'm still going strong.

When I'm feeling fed up, I play my favourite bagpipes CD and I am transported, once again, to the hills outside Glasgow, back to my dear old Granny, and back to the farm. The music brings me so much comfort.

I've recently got together with a new partner, Tony, and we're good companions for each other.

I still visit Sunny's grave every weekend and often, through the sound of the birds and the distant traffic, I can hear his voice.

"Don't let anyone walk over you, Carol."

I am most thankful of all for my wonderful son, his partner and my three beautiful granddaughters. So much of my life has been truly rotten, but with them in my life, I will always feel blessed. With them to support me, my smile will be that much wider and my burden will be so much lighter.

The Convent
Marie Hargreaves
With Ann and Joe Cusack

When a fancy car pulls up outside six-year-old Marie's home in Oldham, in 1959, she is told she is going on holiday...

In fact, she is taken to live in a convent, overseen by a cruel and sadistic nun. There, a horrific ritual of physical, sexual and mental abuse begins.

Marie feels unable to share details of her suffering with anyone. Until years later, when a police investigation is launched, and she realises that the time has finally come to tell the truth...

MIRROR BOOKS

written by Ann and Joe Cusack ...

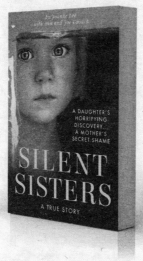

Silent Sisters

Joanne Lee

With Ann and Joe Cusack

A DEADLY SECRET. A HORRIFYING DISCOVERY.

**For over 20 years, Joanne Lee's mother kept the
remains of her newborn babies hidden in her wardrobe.**

Growing up in a chaotic Merseyside household, Joanne suffered neglect and
abusive control while her mother lapsed into a downward spiral. But the
consequences of her mother's messy lifestyle turned out to be far worse than
Joanne could ever have imagined – the family home held a sinister secret.

In Silent Sisters, Joanne, who was falsely accused of murdering her own
baby sister, tells her story for the first time – her struggle to piece together
the truth and to give four babies the proper burial they deserve.

MIRROR BOOKS